C000246784

WALKING IN KENT
VOL II

This tall avenue of beech trees, decimated by the 1987 hurricane, leads to the High Elms estate. (Walk 2)

WALKING IN KENT
VOL II

by

KEV REYNOLDS

CICERONE PRESS
MILNTHORPE, CUMBRIA

© Kev Reynolds 1994
ISBN 1 85284 156 7
A catalogue record for this book is available from the British Library

For my wife - with love

Cicerone guidebooks by the same author:

Walks & Climbs in the Pyrenees	*Walks in the Engadine - Switzerland*
The Valais - Switzerland	*The Jura* (with R.Brian Evans)
The Bernese Alps	*Ticino - Switzerland*
Central Switzerland	*Alpine Pass Route*
Chamonix to Zermatt - the Walker's Haute Route	
Annapurna - a Trekker's Guide	*Walking in Kent*
The Wealdway & The Vanguard Way	*The South Downs Way & The Downs Link*
The Cotswold Way	

Front Cover: The oasts of Hoathly Farm beckon across the fields. *(Walk 25)*

CONTENTS

INTRODUCTION

Spring sunshine bathes the morning, inspiring fresh buds to waken in the apple tree just outside my window. Birds raise their anthem to the new day; heads tilted, their warbling songs are a response to the season's promise. Later, when dew has evaporated and fragrance is drawn from flowers by the sun, confused bees will be at work - as they were yesterday.

It's a season of tremulous excitement.

Throughout the countryside life is erupting with unrestrained vigour as though never before was spring so full. It was, of course. Every spring gives rise to these palpitations of wonder - though we easily forget. Yesterday we were out again, knee-deep in pop-eyed lambs, wandering footpaths along which we could feel the season's pulse bursting through the turf, exploding in hedgerow and woodland shaw, burning from every primrose and celandine-gold bank. Fields tilted on a south-facing slope shaded to dust-brown under the harrow. And our hearts sang.

How better to respond to this or any other season, than to step out into the countryside? Wandering footpaths away from tarmac or concrete is to experience the very heartbeat of nature. Step through the beechwoods and listen to an overpowering peace; gaze from a hilltop and see the land spread before you like a multi-textured blanket, quilted with meadow, spinney or field put to corn. As this is Kent maybe that quilt will consist of orchard, hop garden or vineyard too. And a dazzle of light on water. A farm reservoir, perhaps, or a twisting stream, or a hammer pond where once resounded the clash of new-forged iron but now only the lazy flap of a heron's wings disturbs the hush of a forgotten corner of a much-loved land.

And this is our heritage: acres of gentle-rolling countryside, peaceful and rich in natural beauty. Here, in the "overcrowded" South-East.

Despite considerable pressure placed upon this countryside by developers, councillors and government ministers, by a powerful lobby for ever wider, ever faster roads, for high-speed rail links, out-of-town shopping centres and the like, Kent remains a marvellous county for the walker of footpaths with more than 4000 miles of Rights of Way scoring through an ever-varied, long-cherished landscape.

This book is a guide to some of them.

Forty walks (and suggestions for others) provide a mere sample. But each one is offered in the hope that it will lead to a greater love of this land; for it is only by knowing and loving it that we may hope to protect it from those who seek its exploitation and eventual destruction. Kent is vulnerable. Without question it is among the most heavily pressured of all counties, but still it holds many priceless gems. By walking its footpaths there's an opportunity to discover some of those gems.

A few days ago I walked from just after 11.00am until almost 3.00pm without seeing another human being. This was not in an exotic wilderness on the far side of the world, but in Kent, some twenty miles from the heart of London! That walk is included in this book.

On other occasions I've linked some of these walks into very full days of wandering and never set foot in a village large enough to boast either a pub or a shop. And after a quarter of a century of exploring Kent, I've recently stumbled across hamlets I never knew existed, visited remote redundant churches (some now turned into private homes), strolled through woodlands not shown even on detailed Ordnance Survey maps, and been daily excited by visions of glory.

* * *

The countryside is changing, of course, as it always will. Those who think otherwise have not walked far. Not only does it change with the physical intrusion of man's concrete cancer, but also under the forces of nature. The Great Storm of October 1987 is a potent example of this. But there are other changes inflicted on the land and it is almost inevitable that between active days of walking research and the period during which this book will be in print, alterations to the landscape will affect certain of the routes described. I think of the felling of trees, the enlarging of fields by farmers grubbing out hedgerows (it's still going on), and the changes such as "set-aside" wrought by EC regulations. Some farmers have thrown up their hands in despair and sold large portions of land as golf courses. Others have sought (and gained) diversion orders so sections of footpath alter course. And I can think of at least one walk that will inevitably be slightly re-routed when a proposed school is built on what is at present a green-field site.

Should you find that a section of any walk described has altered dramatically, for one reason or another, I'd appreciate a note giving specific details, and it will be checked for any subsequent edition. Correspondence may be addressed to me c/o the publisher.

As for obstructions to Rights of Way, any problems encountered should be reported to: The Public Rights of Way Manager, Highways and Transportation Department, Kent County Council, Springfield, Maidstone ME14 2LX.

* * *

I am grateful to all those readers of the earlier *Walking in Kent* who wrote with comments regarding routes described in that book, and who urged me to produce another collection. Thanks especially are due to my wife who walked most of these footpaths with me, and to the encouragement, advice and support of Roger Lambert, Access and Recreation Officer for KCC, who is as eager as I am to promote the cause of walking in Kent.

Kev Reynolds
Spring 1994

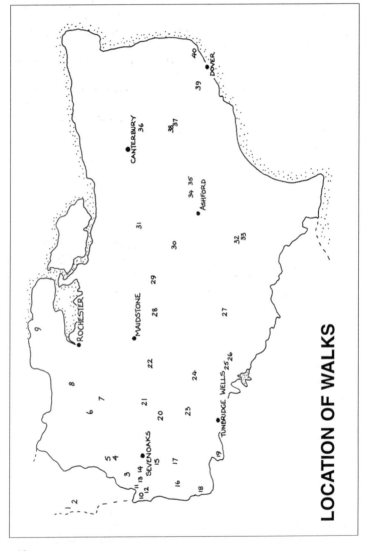

LOCATION OF WALKS

KENT - A WALKER'S COUNTY

This large and complex county may be conveniently divided into four regions dominated by its main geographical features. First the **NORTH DOWNS**. The long chalk ridge that extends in an arc across Kent from its north-western boundary with Surrey, to the majesty of the white cliffs of Dover on the Channel coast, provides an escarpment of visual elegance. Caught within the escarpment gentle vales hold pockets of seclusion, while from the scarp edge views often look out over the great expanse of the Weald. The downland arc is broken in just four places where rivers have formed a breach: north of Sevenoaks by the Darent, near Maidstone where the Medway cuts through, at Wye where the Great Stour has forced a passage en route to Canterbury, and east of Canterbury, thanks to the Little Stour. The main breach is that of the River Medway whose estuary broadens east of Rochester; an estuary speckled with tiny islands. Edging the Medway's estuary is the thumb-like protuberance of the Hoo Peninsular, a low-lying land fringed with marshes where the Thames estuary marks the county's northern limit.

Footpaths explore the low, windy peninsular of Hoo and criss-cross the downs through a surprisingly uncluttered landscape. Perhaps the first major trails in Kent, if not in all of Britain, were those forced along the North Downs by the earliest settlers of these isles when the Weald was still an almost impenetrable forest. The downland crest acted then as a highway; today the North Downs Way traces those ancient routes.

Running parallel to the chalk downs is the **GREENSAND RIDGE**, a succession of ragstone hills that form an inner lining to the North Downs and a wall to the Weald. In places the ridge is very narrow (particularly in the west between the Surrey border and Sevenoaks) and it takes only a few minutes to walk from one side to the other. But what a contrast between north and south! To the north runs the Holmesdale valley with the upthrusting downs above it, while to the south one gazes over a magical spread of countryside with long blue crests forming a far horizon. This southern edge plunges steeply all along the ridge from Crockham Hill to Sevenoaks, and east again, especially beyond Yalding where there is drama in every ridge-top mile. In places this southern slope has been scooped into concave shapes, and in certain areas dramatic landslips have occurred: Crockham Hill and Toys Hill are two that have experienced major hillside disturbances recorded through history.

Some of Kent's finest walking is to be enjoyed along the Greensand Ridge; in and out of woods, across commons deep in bracken or lush with rhododendron, or along bare crests with uninterrupted views to north or south. But it was the Greensand Ridge that caught some of the worst excesses of the 1987 hurricane winds, and as a result lost hundreds of acres of mature woodland. Happily nature is making amends for that loss; wild flowers are exploiting new light, and open views are now to be had that would have been denied to at least two generations of Kentish folk. Along the ridge runs one of Southern England's newest long-distance paths, the Greensand Way.

Then there is **THE WEALD** itself, that vast clay basin containing the Garden of England and which once formed such an obstacle to the Romans. They called it *Anderida*. In those days it was a great forest, parts of which were felled for iron-smelting. Long after the Romans, the Weald became one of the largest iron-making regions in all Europe; today there are hop gardens and wheatfields, orchards and vineyards and meadows flecked with sheep. Agriculture reigns supreme and there are farms everywhere. Some of their buildings add grace to the landscape: oast houses, water mills, tile-hung or weatherboarded cottages, timber-framed hall houses that count among Kent's rich hoard of 24,000 historic buildings handed down with loving care from one generation to another. There are grand stately homes set in vast acres of deer-grazed parkland. There are castles too, with history and romance in every weathered stone. And a few small towns and villages that owe their distinctive architecture to the prosperity of fourteenth century clothmasters.

The Weald has its own series of hills and ridges, some with villages perched atop, like Goudhurst or Bidborough; other areas that are low-lying and heavy underfoot, especially after prolonged rain. And yet again ancient footpaths entice through this garden. Go in spring and rejoice in the blossoms that adorn orchard and hedgerow alike; or in autumn when Midas has transformed each woodland into a halo of burnished gold. Go walking when the hop harvest is in full activity and catch the musky smell that drifts of an evening. At any time, go walking and discover the delights of the Weald. There is no shortage of footpaths, but for those who enjoy an extra-long walk, try the Wealdway which cuts across a corner of the region on its 82-mile journey from Gravesend to Beachy Head.

At the southern end of Kent spreads that strange, level, low-lying region of **ROMNEY MARSH**; land that once was sea. Bordered by a modest green slope with the Royal Military Canal acting as a protective moat, the marsh is a jigsaw of pasture outlined by a grid of dye-straight drainage ditches. All seems bent to the horizon; ragged hedgerows, wind-brushed trees, even the towers of weathered churches appear to huddle low against the sea-breeze. It's a land of deep mystery, a land with its own peculiar charm, its own personal history. Strange to think, as we wander its footpaths, that sheep graze today where once the tides gathered. Where flowers bloom now, the Danes once sailed their longships on raiding parties that brought terror to the men and women of Kent. The Saxon Shore Way traces the edge of this ancient coastline at the end of its epic 135-mile journey from Gravesend round the county's rim to gentle Rye across the border in Sussex. But there are other, less-demanding, walks to be had throughout Romney Marsh, accompanied by the lazy bleating of marshland sheep, and by the glint of sunlight on one of a hundred or more watercourses.

NOTES FOR WALKERS

Walking provides year-round pleasure, for each season has its own special appeal, its own unique flavour. Tackling footpaths described in this book will require no specialised equipment, but it is important to use comfortable, well-fitting footwear. Conditions underfoot vary as often as the weather, and while it is probably only country dwellers familiar with their locality who will know what is suitable footwear at any given time, it is essential that whatever you choose is comfortable, waterproof and well-fitting in order to avoid sore feet or blisters.

Choose clothing suitable for the season, and be flexible enough to take account of changeable weather. What you wear ought to give protection against high or tangled vegetation as well as from crops that may be damp after rain. For summer walking shorts may be fine along certain footpaths, but often brambles or nettles tend to stray onto a path, and in such cases you'll be glad of the protection afforded by long trousers. Light, inexpensive overtrousers can be particularly useful.

If you're unused to walking, consider carrying a pack of plasters in case of blisters, or for the odd scratch or two. An Ordnance Survey map (so long as you know how to use it!) will be useful should you become lost - and also to add to the walk's interest by enabling you to identify distant features. A note with regard to specific sheets required is given for each walk. On a full day in the countryside I always carry a few sandwiches and an apple for lunch, as I'd much rather picnic beneath a tree with a view than stop at a pub. However, pubs are noted where they occur, for the benefit of those with a preference for liquid refreshment. Most offer a selection of snacks and bar meals, but it should be pointed out that not all landlords welcome ramblers - and having seen how much clay can be picked up on walking boots after a mile of Wealden wandering, I have a degree of sympathy with them! Be prepared to leave your boots outside, or wear poly bags over them when entering a pub. Mention of any public house or cafe in this guide must not be taken as an endorsement of its services.

It is assumed that anyone setting out on a walk in the countryside will be a lover of that countryside. And yet almost daily we discover pieces of litter where only walkers go. Since litter is one of civilisation's less laudable offshoots, we all have a responsibility to do our bit towards reducing its impact. No longer should we be passive in our attitude towards it, but instead act positively by taking home not only our own rubbish, but a few items left by others. That way we can begin to clean up our countryside. Maybe then walkers will shame certain farmers into cleaning up their own rubbish - so that one day we may enjoy the countryside without the sight of fertiliser bags snagged in the hedgerows and ditches, and items of once-expensive machinery rusting in a field.

Paths may not always be abundantly clear on the ground, but directions given in this guidebook should enable you to follow the correct route without difficulty. Where paths lead through a field of growing crops, please walk in single file to minimise the damage. And remember, hay is an important crop too. Treat fields of long grass as you would those of ripening wheat, and use the stiles or gates provided to cross hedges and fences.

Kent is a sheep-raising county, and many of the walks go through meadows with flocks grazing. Take care not to panic them, especially when ewes are in lamb in early spring. Keep dogs on a lead and under close control at all times. Farmers have a right to shoot dogs found worrying animals.

Some of our walks traverse golf courses, and when on these outings you should keep extra vigilant, especially when crossing a fairway.

USING THE GUIDE

Maps:

Sketch maps accompanying walks described have been produced to give an overview of each route, but are no real alternative to Ordnance Survey maps which obviously provide more accurate detail of the area. At the head of each walk a note of the OS maps covering the actual route is given. The Pathfinder series give plenty of detail, including field boundaries - although these are not always entirely accurate due to changes made since the last survey. Pathfinder maps are published at a scale of 1:25,000 ($2^{1}/_2$" = 1 mile).

The Landranger series covers a much wider area, but with appreciably less detail at a scale of 1:50,000 ($1^{1}/_4$" = 1 mile).

Grid references are occasionally quoted to help locate a given position on the OS map. Each map is divided into a series of vertical and horizontal lines, creating a "grid" (the British National Grid). These lines are provided with a number, which is quoted at the top, bottom or sides of the sheet. Numbers increase from left to right for vertical lines (known as "eastings"), and from bottom to top for horizontal lines ("northings").

In order to identify an exact point on the map from a given grid reference, take the first two digits from the number quoted. These refer to the "eastings" line on the map. The third digit is estimated in tenths of the square moving eastward from that line. Next, take the fourth and fifth digits which refer to the "northings" line, while the final digit is that number of tenths of the square reading up the sheet. Grid references quoted are the same on matching 1:25,000 and 1:50,000 sheets.

Times and Distances:

Distances quoted in the text, although measured on the map, are approximations only, but are reasonably accurate. (Note that heights are quoted on OS maps in metres and not feet, and grid lines are spaced one kilometre apart.)

Allow between 2 and 2¹/₂ miles per hour for your walk, without prolonged stops. Following wet weather when conditions may be heavy underfoot, one's pace will undoubtedly be a little slower, as it will when accompanied by young children or inexperienced walkers.

A Countryside Glossary:

Certain words used in the text may not be immediately familiar, so the following brief glossary is offered as explanation.

coppice an area of trees, usually hazel or sweet chestnut, that are intermittently cut to a stump from which new shoots will grow, thereby enabling a regular harvest of timber to be taken.

headland the edge of a field that is difficult for the farmer to plough, and is therefore often left rough. It provides a natural habitat for numerous small mammals, and allows the walker to ease around the field without damaging crops.

pollard similar to coppicing, but here trees are cut about six feet from the ground. Some very old woods and forests show fine examples, and on a few of our walks pollarded willows are seen. Very little pollarding is done these days.

shaw a strip of woodland, usually separating two fields.

* * *

Finally, please observe the Country Code:

 1: Enjoy the countryside and respect its life and work.
 2: Guard against all risk of fire.
 3: Fasten all gates.

4:     Keep dogs under close control.
5:     Keep to public paths across farmland.
6:     Use gates and stiles to cross fences, hedges and walls.
7:     Leave livestock, crops and machinery alone.
8:     Take litter home.
9:     Help to keep all water clean.
10:    Protect wildlife, plants and trees.
11:    Take special care on country roads.
12:    Make no unnecessary noise.

It was Octavia Hill, that indomitable champion of the countryside and co-founder of the National Trust (who spent some of her happiest days along the Greensand Ridge and who is buried in Crockham Hill churchyard), whose words at the turn of the century sum up the spirit of the Country Code:

"Let the grass growing for hay be respected, let the primrose roots be left in their loveliness in the hedges, the birds unmolested and the gates shut. If those who frequented country places would consider those who live there, they would better deserve, and more often retain, the rights and privileges they enjoy."

Tucked below the North Downs, just outside Trottiscliffe, the Coldrum Stones mark the site of a Neolithic burial chamber. (Walk 7)

North Kent

THE DOWNS, DARENT AND HOO PENINSULAR

With London's land-hungry sprawl edging ever outward, northern Kent seems destined to fight a rear-guard action against being swallowed completely. Motorways score through it and across it; a never-ceasing drone of traffic that, on still days, can be heard for miles. However, contained within the North Downs escarpment stretching east from the Surrey border to the Medway gap near Rochester, there lies a surprisingly remote patch of rural tranquillity where the wanderer of footpaths can find peace as well as a natural, timeless beauty. In this back-of-beyond narrow lanes twist among nest-filled hedgerows, linking one little hamlet with another. Better still, footpaths and bridleways entice over gentle rolling downland, through neat vales and into woods and spinneys alive with birdsong.

The historic small town of Westerham, with its statues of Churchill and Wolfe on the green, lies in the Holmesdale valley between the North Downs and the Greensand Ridge, right on the Surrey border. On the downs above it Betsom's Hill is Kent's highest. Running east from Betsom's Hill the steep scarp face of the North Downs presents a considerable wall, when viewed from the valley, but this is broken near Chevening by the broad slice of the Darent gap.

Wedged between the Surrey border and the Darent's valley this block of land eases northward to the Greater London boundary. Yet countryside persists almost as far as Bromley and Orpington, and it takes only a few short minutes to escape the suburbs in order to exchange housing estates for wood-crowded hills and sunken coombes where rabbit, badger and fox roam free. This is countryside known and loved by Charles Darwin (1809-82), the great Victorian naturalist who for forty years lived at Downe, where he wrote his controversial work, *The Origin of Species*. (See Walk 2.)

Where the Darent has forced a route through the chalk downs between Chevening and Otford its valley is a real gem - at least that which lies between Otford and Farningham. The Darent itself is a modest stream, but what it lacks in volume it compensates with character. This is a stream that knows orchard and hop garden, that occasionally spills over onto low-lying water-meadows, or meanders on a summer's day beneath dipping willows. At Shoreham it flows past The Water House, where the artist Samuel Palmer once lived; at Lullingstone it feeds a dazzling lake below a mansion with a Queen Anne façade, then slides by the remains of a magnificent Roman villa. At Eynsford it lures paddling children to a picturesque ford, and long ago formed the moat to a Norman castle.

Palmer found inspiration in the Darent valley. Today walkers can do likewise, not only with routes described in this book, but also along the 15-mile Darent Valley Path (Sevenoaks to Dartford) and circular walks from it, while at Lullingstone Park Visitor Centre guided walks are arranged and interpretive leaflets and guidebooks on sale to encourage a positive use of this much-loved rural oasis.

To the east of the Darent gap the North Downs swell to full height once more, but offer a scarp face to both the west and the south. Again, as with the downland block west of the Darent, this wedge of countryside, with the M20 its eastern limit, also slopes northward. Here are more delightful unfussed coombes, little knuckle indents of valleys devoid of streams but with a few remote farm ponds sunken in their upper folds. Woods and spinneys attract jackdaws to their branches; green woodpeckers break the silence of morning with their maniacal laughter, and old man's beard (wild clematis) fluffs each winter hedgerow.

Beyond the M20 the North Downs escarpment continues in a natural unbroken sweep as far as the breach forced by the Medway. Its northern limit is crowded by Thames-side towns and their satellite villages that creep into the countryside. But the southern edge is largely timber and chalk and with big views into the Weald. Trosley Country Park is a honeypot perched on the scarp edge where crowds gather at weekends and bright summer days, but these are soon swallowed by a maze of paths that venture through the woods and onto steep open meadows hanging from the slope. Just below this slope stand the Coldrum Stones, the remains of a long barrow or burial chamber, dating back some 4000 years.

Apart from such expanding communities as Meopham and New Ash Green, "inland" villages and tiny hamlets huddle seemingly lost to the outside world: Ridley, Fairseat, Hodsoll Street. There's Harvel, and Luddesdown where a house next to the church has been continuously lived in for at least 900 years, and nearby Dode (not recognised by the Ordnance Survey) whose parishioners were lost to the Black Death 600 years ago. Twisting lanes do their best to explore this heartland, but footpaths do a far better job and from them it's hard to believe that towns and cities are only a comparatively short drive away.

Spreading to the north-east of the downs, and caught between the estuaries of Thames and Medway, the low-lying Hoo Peninsular provides a very different prospect. Dickens, who lived for many years at Gadshill Place, Higham, knew the region well and described its bleakness in *Great Expectations*: "...my own marsh country, flat and monotonous, and with a dim horizon, while the winding river turned and turned and everything else seemed stranded and still". A great walker, Dickens of course was an even greater novelist who spun a marvellous evocation of the fog-wreathed marshes that border the Thames. Bleak it most certainly can be, but Hoo is not without its charm, and the marshes and mudflats that edge this raw projection of land can sparkle as brightly as anywhere in Kent under the influence of sunshine. It's a sparsely-populated region with a sprinkling of farms dotted about a broad landscape. Industry, in the shape of oil refineries, has done its best to ruin some of the views, but he would be blind indeed who could not see the visual pleasures that still abound.

High Halstow is by no means high, yet it appears so when seen from Cooling and Halstow Marshes. The village is crowned by woodland on Northward Hill where the RSPB has a major reserve in which Britain's largest heronry is sited. Bluebells spread a rich carpet in spring, and footpaths lead to long views over the northern flats where the Thames glides between Kent and Essex. Throughout the marshes ducks and geese gather; waders stalk mudflats deserted by an ebbing tide and one can amble for hours without being disturbed by human activity. Only the birds gather in crowds.

The Saxon Shore Way is still in its infancy as it meanders

through, while a series of circular walks based on that long-distance route explore Shorne and Higham Marshes and are treated to a combined booklet and route card published by Kent County Council. Hoo then has its undoubted appeal for the naturalist and wanderer of footpaths, and trails known to Dickens still link lonely churches, farms and small villages. As they have for centuries.

* * *

NORTH KENT COUNTRY PARKS AND OPEN SPACES:

1:   Hollows Wood, Badgers Mount: 145 acres of sweet chestnut woodland divided by the M25 link-road to Orpington. To the east of the A224.

2:   Andrews Wood, Badgers Mount: 185 acres of mixed woodland; picnic area. South of Hollows Wood.

3:   Lullingstone Park: 300 acres of woods and parkland; Visitor Centre, refreshments. Access from minor road linking A225 with Shoreham. (See Walk 5.)

4:   Joyden's Wood, Dartford: 320 acres of woodland; good opportunities for walks. South of junction of A2018 and A223.

5:   Beacon Wood Country Park: 70 acres of mixed deciduous woodland; disused claypit site of interest to naturalists. Near Bean, south of A2 and south-east of Dartford.

6:   Trosley Country Park: 160 acres of woodland on the southern edge of the North Downs; Visitor Centre, waymarked walks, fine views. Access via A227 south of Culverstone Green. Near Vigo village. (See Walk 7.)

7:   Holly Hill Wood: 32 acres of woodland on one of the highest parts of the North Downs; fine views over the Medway valley. Access via minor road running west of A228 at Snodland.

8:   Camer Country Park: 46 acres of mature parkland; refreshments. North-east of Meopham, access via B2009. (See Walk 8.)

9:   Shorne Wood Country Park: 174 acres of woodland, heath and wetland; Information Centre. North of Cobham, access near Cobham/Shorne interchange off A2.

WALK 1: KESTON - BERRY'S GREEN - WESTERHAM

Distance:	7 miles
Maps:	OS Pathfinder TQ 46/56 Orpington and TQ 45/55 Sevenoaks & Westerham 1:25,000
	OS Landranger 187 Dorking Reigate & Crawley 1:50,000
Start:	Keston Ponds (Grid ref: 419640)
Access:	On the A233, 1½ miles south of Bromley Common. Keston and Westerham are served by bus from Bromley.
Parking:	Public car park by Keston Ponds.
Refreshments:	Pubs near Berry's Green and in Westerham. Cafes in Westerham.

Although it lies within the administrative district of the London Borough of Bromley, Keston retains a rural flavour and provides a springboard from which much fine countryside may be explored. This particular walk traces a north-south course through fields and woodlands, over neat hills and along a groove of tight little vales to the edge of the North Downs, then plunges into the Holmesdale valley at Westerham. Footpaths are well-defined almost throughout its length. As a linear walk a return to the start could be made by bus from Westerham. Alternatively, have a car stationed at either end.

* * *

A footpath (waymarked Farnborough Circular Walk) begins in the car park just south of Keston Ponds and heads parallel to the A233 for a short distance before bearing left and crossing the road. It now leads through woodland alongside the boundary fence of unseen Holwood House, and soon arrives at the Wilberforce Oak, an ancient but now-dead tree noted as the site where in 1788 William Wilberforce announced to Prime Minister Pitt his intention to bring before Parliament a Bill to abolish the slave trade. A memorial seat is placed here to enjoy the view south.

The path crosses a driveway and goes between fields to reach the junction of Downe Road and Shire Lane. Bear left along Downe Road for about 150 yards, then take a footpath on the right. This leads along the right-hand boundary of a field, at the far side of

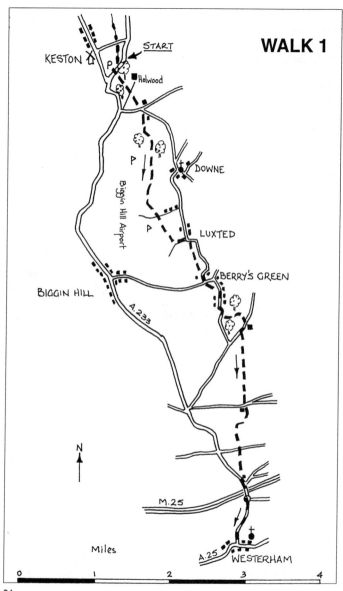

WALK 1

START

KESTON

Holwood

Biggin Hill Airport

DOWNE

LUXTED

BERRY'S GREEN

BIGGIN HILL

A.233

N

M.25

Miles

A.25   WESTERHAM

0   1   2   3   4

which bear left and go up a slope alongside a fence, then over a stile on the right. Cross this field to its far left-hand corner, enter woods and come to a junction of paths. Take the right-hand option, effectively going straight ahead. (The left-hand path goes off to Downe; see Walk 2.)

On emerging from the trees enter a sloping field and cross at mid-height to a stile in a line of trees dividing this from the next field. Continue ahead, maintaining direction along the top edge of fields bordering a golf course, then enter a patch of woodland scrub in which the path soon curves left and rises uphill. When it forks bear right along a row of cypress trees and come to a narrow lane serving the Clubhouse. Cross over and through some metal bars continue among more woodland scrub. At a 4-way path junction go straight ahead towards Luxted. Leave the scrub, walk alongside a tee (beware golf balls), then resume among rough grass and scrub once more, before walking along the edge of a small field and through trees to another narrow lane in Luxted (Grid ref: 432603).

Bear left to a road and a telephone kiosk. Turn right and a few paces later go right again into the farmyard of Luxted Farm. Cross a stile and walk ahead along the left-hand edge of a small field, and continue on the edge of two more fields linked by stiles. (Ignore a path heading left halfway along the last of these fields.) Leave this last field in front of a white house and join a road. Walk ahead until reaching a T junction (Jail Lane) with another telephone kiosk. (A short distance to the right is a pub.)

Directly ahead are two signposted paths. Take the surfaced left-hand option leading to Berry's Green. Turn right on a road and walk along it for about 400 yards. Soon after negotiating a double-bend, leave the road on a footpath heading left to New Barn Lane (Grid ref: 438588). At first it descends steeply among trees, then rises more gently over a hill to a junction of paths. Bear right, still in trees, and slope down to a field. Cross this to New Barn Farm. Bear right on the lane and 50 yards later take a footpath on the left which heads along a delightful valley.

Maintain direction along the edge of two or three fields, then come to a stile and a choice of paths. Continue ahead among scrub across a sloping meadow, on the far side of which cross another stile into an open field. Walk through it (woods on the right) and come to crossing paths (field gates and stiles on either side). Continue ahead, now rising uphill half-left to a stile on the skyline in a row of trees. Continue up to the brow of a hill. There is no sign of a path on the ground. Maintain direction over the highest part of the field to another stile on the opposite boundary. This leads into yet another field with a farm seen on the far side.

Cross a lane in front of Stud Cottage (Grid ref: 444570), and walk along a track that goes down the left-hand side of the house. This leads between fields, then forks. Take the right-hand branch, in effect straight ahead, and begin to slope down towards the edge of the North Downs escarpment. Come to the North Downs Way (1), bear right and wander downhill with the Holmesdale valley spread below and the scragged ridgeline of greensand hills rising on the far side.

Descend a series of wood-braced steps and turn right along the upper edge of a large field. On coming to the scrub boundary bear left and walk down the field edge to a narrow lane. Cross over and follow the left-hand headland of another field. After passing beneath power lines the way becomes a grass track between hedgerows, narrows to a path, then exits to the A233 by the side of a house (Grid ref: 445554). Cross with care and turn left on the roadside footpath, go over the M25 and on into Westerham. (Note: before coming to the motorway you'll pass a bus stop used by buses going to Bromley via Keston. There are other bus stops for this route in Westerham High Street.)

Items of interest:

1: North Downs Way. One of the best-known of our National Trails, this long distance route was designated by the Countryside Commission in 1978. It runs from Farnham in Surrey to Dover, with an alternative spur via Canterbury, and is 141 miles long. KCC has produced a handy booklet; *The North Downs Way - A Users Guide.*

WALK 2: DOWNE - CUDHAM - HAZELWOOD - DOWNE

Distance:	7 miles
Maps:	OS Pathfinder TQ 46/56 Orpington, TQ 45/55 Sevenoaks & Westerham 1:25,000 OS Landranger 187 Dorking, Reigate & Crawley, 188 Maidstone & The Weald of Kent 1:50,000
Start:	Downe Church (Grid ref: 433616)
Access:	By signposted minor road heading east from A233 south of Keston.
Parking:	With discretion in the village.
Refreshments:	Pubs in Downe and Cudham (off route).

Noted beyond the parish boundaries as the village in which Charles Darwin lived, Downe has an attractive heart where the church, two pubs and a number of pretty cottages line converging roads. These roads are little more than narrow country lanes that delve into the countryside without seeing much beyond primrose banks and high hedgerows. Yet there is a good selection of footpaths and bridleways which explore open meadows, secretive coombes and bluebell woods that make up this downland on the very rim of suburbia. Though Bromley and Orpington are never far away, and at times can be seen filling a distant view, it is rural peace that prevails. This walk makes the most of that peace by linking a number of those footpaths, bridleways and green lanes, some of which are waymarked sections of circular walks promoted by Bromley Council.

* * *

Begin by walking south-westward away from the parish church along Luxted Road, soon passing the village Baptist Church on the left. About 50 yards beyond this bear left on a footpath signposted to Cudham. Initially a walled path between houses, it soon comes to a field. Follow the left-hand boundary, cross a stile and turn right. (Another path continues ahead.) Now keep along the right-hand side of a field to a swing gate in the far boundary, so to enter another field. Continue directly ahead, but note the large white house on the right, beyond the hedge. This is Down House (1), Darwin's home for forty years, now open to the public (Grid ref: 432612).

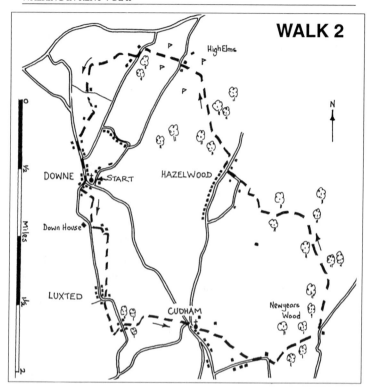

At the far side of the field bear left towards Downe Court, cross a stile onto a driveway and in a few paces turn right and walk in front of the farmhouse to another stile. The way continues, well-signed for the Leaves Green Circular Walk, round two sides of a large field, then straight ahead all the way to the hamlet of Luxted, which is finally reached by way of a narrow path alongside a garden boundary. Come to a road, cross a little to the right and go through the entrance to Luxted Farm (Grid ref: 434603).

Pass to the left of the farmhouse, cross a stile and walk ahead along the left-hand edge of three fields. Midway along the third of these turn left on an enclosed footpath (part of the Cudham Circular Walk) which leads to another narrow road (a continuation of that crossed in Luxted), with the footpath continuing directly ahead. This leads into a woodland that is bright with bluebells in spring, then descends a long flight of steps into a valley. Leave the wood and continue straight across an open field with Cudham church spire seen on the brow of the hill ahead. The way steepens and reaches Church Hill at a junction of roads. Bear left, then right to gain the flint-walled church of St Peter and St Paul. (If refreshments are needed, turn right at the crossroads for a short distance to find the village pub.)

Walk through the churchyard and into a playing field, which is crossed half right to a continuing footpath in the far boundary. This path is enclosed with the wall boundary of Angas Home on the left, and it leads to open fields. Aim half-right and cross a series of fields (linked by stiles) to gain a narrow country road opposite Pole Barn Farm (Grid ref: 451597). Turn left, and about 50 yards beyond Cacket's Farm, as the road veers sharply to the right, cross a stile on the left and go over a narrow field to the edge of a wood and a 3-way path junction. Bear left on a footpath which hugs the lower edge of the wood, then eases to the right and climbs through it on what can be a very muddy trail in winter.

Eventually come to another narrow lane opposite a cottage. Do not go onto the lane, but bear left on a woodland track signposted to Green Street Green and Pratt's Bottom. Pass through a coppiced area and come to a field gate with a stile. Walk directly ahead across a field to a woodland shaw on the far side. Another stile leads into this shaw which goes to High Wood. On reaching the wood (beautifully carpeted with wood anemones in springtime) take the left-hand bridleway which eases down the woodland edge, then goes through a narrow valley before rising to Broom Wood.

Continue through Broom Wood, then along a shaw linking it with Foxberry Wood and a path junction. Take the right-hand bridleway (Cudham Circular Walk) that rises between fields, winds over a modest hilltop, and eventually reaches Snag Lane (Grid ref: 451617). Walk directly ahead on this narrow lane to a T junction at Hazelwood. Bear right, then a few paces later go left into a field with two footpaths signposted. Bear right alongside a hedge running parallel to the road. (For a shorter return to Downe take the alternative path.) At the far side of the field go through a swing gate and turn left on a bridleway signposted to High Elms (2).

Following wet weather this bridleway can be extremely muddy, but entering Cuckoo Wood a footpath is fenced to one side of the bridleway, which is a marked improvement. The path rises uphill, goes through a splendid avenue of tall, elegant beech trees and comes to a golf course. Continue ahead eventually reaching a lane near High Elms Clockhouse. Cross over and take the footpath (not the bridleway) which rises over a further section of golf course, passes through a small woodland and comes to another lane opposite North End Farm. Bear left and walk along North End Lane for about 100 yards, then turn right into Bogey Lane, a narrow track, or green lane. After a short distance leave the track in favour of a footpath which follows on the left.

From the footpath pleasant views gaze off to the right over a fold of hillside to green meadows and woods hiding the conurbation of Farnborough, Orpington and Bromley a very short distance away. The field boundary curves left, the footpath with it. Rejoin the track near an electricity pylon and soon come to an extremely narrow lane. The footpath continues directly ahead, but behind at this point is a view which includes the southern aspect of palatial Holwood House (see Walk 1), designed by Decimus Burton.

The footpath cuts through a field, and leaves it near the far corner by a gap in the hedge. Bear right, cross a stile to the left of a solitary house and walk ahead along an enclosed footpath which leads to Rookery Road. Turn left and walk on to Downe Church.

Items of interest:

1: Down House. Charles Darwin (1809-1882) lived and worked here for 40 years, and wrote his controversial *The Origin of Species* (published 1859) in the study. Of the house, he wrote: "After fruitless searches in Surrey and elsewhere, we found this house and purchased it. I was pleased with the diversified appearance of the vegetation proper to a chalk district...and still more pleased with the extreme quietness and rusticity of the place." Down House is open to the public.

2: High Elms. Formerly home to Lord Avebury (Sir John Lubbock) and his heirs, the estate is now owned by the London Borough of Bromley. It has a field study centre, golf course, and lots of open spaces and woodlands.

St Botolph's church at Chevening, at the start of Walk 3

WALK 3: CHEVENING - KNOCKHOLT POUND - CHEVENING

Distance:	4 miles
Maps:	OS Pathfinder TQ 45/55 Sevenoaks & Westerham 1:25,000
	OS Landranger 188 Maidstone & The Weald of Kent 1:50,000
Start:	St Botolph's church, Chevening (Grid ref: 489577)
Access:	By way of a minor road heading north-west from B2211 1¼ miles north of Sundridge on A25.
Parking:	By the church.
Refreshments:	None.

Situated at the foot of the North Downs about three miles north-west of Sevenoaks (as the crow flies), Chevening is a small hamlet grouped in front of the attractive church of St Botolph, with stately Chevening House partially hidden from view at the end of a private drive. The Chevening estate includes a great sweep of parkland leading to the wall of the downs. From the southern slope of those downs, as from the crest, lovely views overlook not only the house, but the broad Holmesdale valley beyond, and east across the Darent gap to the continuing North Downs fading blue with distance. Despite the close proximity of the M25 Chevening gathers an air of peaceful seclusion, an oasis of sanity to contrast the scourge of motorway madness.

This short walk is not difficult, but there's a long uphill section that could be slippery after rain. In late winter the upper woods are bright with great swathes of snowdrops; in springtime delicate shades of green come to the trees as leaves open to a new season, while in autumn pheasants strut everywhere.

*   *   *

Wander through the churchyard to its eastern side, then bear left to take a footpath leading between hedgerows towards the North Downs. It's an easy, gentle beginning, with parkland of the

Leaving ancient Luddesdown, the path rises over a hill on the way to Great Buckland

On the outskirts of Stansted the walk passes lovely thatched, timber-framed Malt House *(Walk 6)*
From Gillhams Farm views look towards the North Downs *(Walk 11)*

WALK 3

KNOCKHOLT POUND

North Downs Way

KNOCKHOLT

Park House

START

Chevening House   CHEVENING

M.25

N

Miles

0   ½   1   2

Chevening estate on the left. Drawing near a cottage, note a stile on the left; this is used on the return journey. Soon after this pass a very old yew tree, also on the left. The path begins to rise with a pleasant green coombe ahead to the right - and a fine view back to Chevening House (1). Maintain direction, cross a stile and go uphill beside Minny Wood, the gradient now a little more demanding. Gain the crest of the downs and a drive by a cottage. Just beyond this bear left on the North Downs Way.

The path now hugs the left-hand headland of a succession of fields alongside woods. After bearing right, still beside the woods, pass a walled gateway and then turn left over a stile on the continuing North Downs Way. On reaching a narrow country road wander down it for about a third of a mile, then go left on a rough driveway by Keepers Cottage. This leads through woods. Out of the trees cross a stile and descend on the edge of a field with the Holmesdale valley spread out below, then with Chevening House

33

seen ahead.

With storm-battered woodland on the left come to a swing gate. Go through it and bear left, then right over a stile. Along the edge of parkland cross a private estate drive leading to Chevening House, and continue on the other side of the fence. Cross a second driveway and at the end of the next field section rejoin the outward path. Turn right and return to Chevening church.

Items of interest:
1: Chevening House. This seventeenth-century mansion was bequeathed to the nation on the death of the 7th Earl of Stanhope in 1967, together with a £250,000 endowment for its upkeep. Initially occupied by Prince Charles, it then passed to the government as the country residence of a senior minister. It is generally used by the Chancellor of the Exchequor.

WALK 4: SHOREHAM - ROMNEY STREET - SHOREHAM

Distance:	5¹/₂ miles
Maps:	OS Pathfinder TQ 46/56 Orpington 1:25,000
	OS Landranger 188 Maidstone & The Weald of Kent 1:50,000
Start:	Church of St Peter & St Paul, Shoreham (Grid ref: 524616)
Access:	Shoreham is reached via the A225, 3 miles north of Sevenoaks. The village is served by British Rail.
Parking:	With discretion in the village.
Refreshments:	Pubs in Shoreham and Romney Street (150yds off route)

"Everything connected with the village in those happy times," wrote the nineteenth-century artist Samuel Palmer of the seven years he lived in Shoreham, "seemed wrapped about with a sentiment of cosy quiet antiquity, full of association that carried you far back into the pastoral life of Merry England years ago." There's something of that association today, for the Darent valley in which Shoreham nestles is a surprisingly unspoilt vale

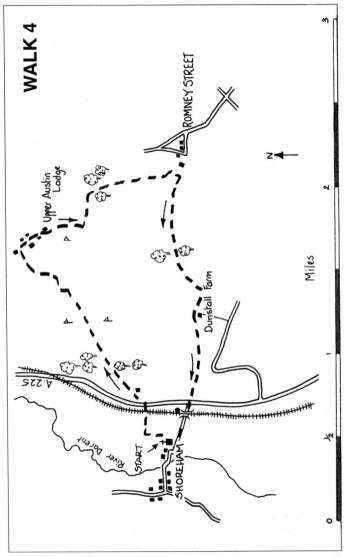

WALK 4

ROMNEY STREET

Upper Austin Lodge

Dunstall Farm

A.225

River Darent

START

SHOREHAM

N

Miles

0   ½   1   2   3

35

caught within the embrace of two spurs of the North Downs, one of which is explored on this walk.

Shoreham features only at the start and finish of this walk, for the Darent is soon deserted in order to cross the eastern wall of the downs, there to enter a charming hidden valley that will come as a great surprise to newcomers to the area. Take a picnic lunch and give time to absorb its tranquil nature. Recently this valley has been adopted as a golf course; yet tranquillity remains. There are several steep sections of path to contend with, and it should be noted that near the crest of the downs the footpath enters a firing range. If it is in use, you'll probably know well in advance of setting out by the sound of firing; but in any case a red flag will be flying if it is unsafe to proceed.

* * *

Approach from the heart of the village and pass through Shoreham churchyard to its eastern side, then leave by a swing gate leading into a field. Turn left and walk along the field edge with the North Downs rising on both sides of the valley. Come to the end of the field and a crossing path, bear right and soon after cross the railway line to arrive beside the A225. Cross the road with care and turn left. About 30 yards later bear right over a stile and half-left through a field to an area of woodland scrub leading to a drive below a house. Cross the drive and follow the path which slants up the hillside among trees. It becomes very steep towards the top of the slope, then enters a firing range marked by a notice board and a flagpole. If a red flag is flying do not proceed until advised by a sentry that it is safe to do so.

Gaining the crest of the downs come to a crossing track and turn left, then bear right on the continuing path rising gently, then along the edge of some trees. The way passes through woods and emerges to fields near a second flagpole. From the woodland corner the path proceeds straight across the field ahead, in effect making for the far corner. A few paces south of the corner enter woods again and begin a steep descent among yew trees.

Leaving the woods the path emerges in a surprisingly peaceful valley on the edge of a golf course. Continue down the slope alongside a hedge, and 100 yards later bear left and walk through the valley to reach a large dutch barn (Grid ref: 541631). By the barn turn right on a farm drive among houses and farm buildings, and follow this to Upper Austin Lodge. Continue, now on a track heading through the golf course in an eastern groove of the valley. Remain on this track until reaching a sign directing the footpath left towards Lower Wood which lines the downland slope. Enter the woods and turn right, then veer left to slant up the hillside. Having gained a little height the way then contours along the hillside among silver birch trees, leaves the woods and continues on the upper edge of meadowland aiming towards the head of the valley.

Remain on the edge of the meadowland as it curves to the right near Romney Street Farm, and come to a stile on the left. (For refreshments, cross the stile and in 150 yards come to The Fox and Hounds pub in the hamlet of Romney Street.) The continuing walk does not cross the stile, however, but instead bears right towards a line of trees with big views over the valley ahead. Descend beyond the trees and cross a shoulder of Round Hill where there are stiles on either side of a track. Cross both stiles and continue steeply downhill into another lovely valley groove used by golfers. Rise on the other side to enter woods, then leave them to go half-left across the corner of a hilltop field. Maintain direction over the next field, then join a crossing track. Turn right to Dunstall Farm (Grid ref: 535614).

In the farmyard veer right then left past some barns, cross another field towards more trees on the lip of the downs. Just after entering Dunstall Woods there is a crossing track. Go straight over this and descend (steeply in places on a long line of steps) into the Darent valley. Cross the A225 opposite Shoreham Station and wander down the road next to it into Shoreham village.

WALK 5: LULLINGSTONE PARK - UPPER AUSTIN LODGE - SHOREHAM - LULLINGSTONE

Distance:	6 miles
Maps:	OS Pathfinder TQ 46/56 Orpington 1:25,000
	OS Landranger 188 Maidstone & The Weald of Kent 1:50,000
Start:	Lullingstone Park Visitor Centre (Grid ref: 526638)
Access:	Via Castle Road, off A225, ½ mile south of Eynsford Station.
Parking:	At the Visitor Centre.
Refreshments:	Cafe at the Visitor Centre; pubs in Eynsford and Shoreham.

On this walk there are rich contrasts between the flat-bottomed Darent valley and the steep-walled downs; the cheerful song of the stream, with its birds and shading trees, and a dry scoop of downland meadow where no surface water flows. (Part of this route reverses a section of Walk 4.) History lingers along the Darent with the ruins of Lullingstone Roman Villa, as well as Lullingstone Castle, an historic mansion with a turreted gatehouse. In addition there's The Water House in Shoreham where the great English Romantic painter Samuel Palmer once lived.

Lullingstone Park Visitor Centre is managed by Sevenoaks District Council. In it there are natural history displays, a cafe and a shop selling a variety of walks leaflets and guides, as well as books with a local countryside interest. Throughout the year guided walks are arranged from the Centre. Various walks begin from the car park, as does ours.

*   *   *

At the car park entrance a signpost directs a footpath downstream to Lullingstone Castle. It leads along the left bank of the Darent, which at this point flows parallel to a lake on whose northern shore is the large red-brick Lullingstone Castle (1) standing among trim lawns and fine trees. Continue beyond the lake to pass the turreted gatehouse (refreshments available when the castle is open), now walking along a narrow metalled lane for about a third of a mile. Come to Lullingstone Roman Villa (2), which is contained in an ugly

WALK 5

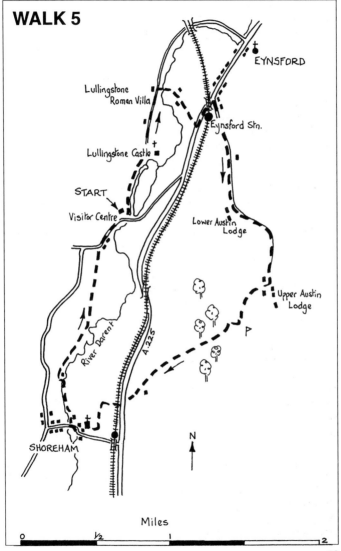

Lullingstone Roman Villa

EYNSFORD

Eynsford Stn.

Lullingstone Castle

START

Visitor Centre

Lower Austin Lodge

Upper Austin Lodge

P

River Darent

A-225

N

SHOREHAM

Miles

0   ½   1   2

green corrugated building on the left. (The Villa remains are well worth a visit, if you have time.)

Bear right opposite the Roman Villa (Grid ref: 530651) on a track heading for New Barn Farm. It crosses the Darent, passes an attractive flint cottage and the farm, and continues to the A225. Cross with care and bear left on the original road (now a slip road); when this ends continue ahead to pass beneath a railway bridge and turn sharp right on a road to Eynsford Station. Walk past the station and along Upper Austin Lodge Road.

This narrow road serves a couple of farms and a golf course, and leads through a delightful valley contained within gentle projecting spurs of the North Downs. Keep on the road for 1^1/$_2$ miles, passing a large house (Chalkhurst) on the left, and several hundred yards later Lower Austin Lodge Farm on the right. The left-hand hillside is covered with typical chalkland scrub, with woods consisting largely of yew crowning the slope.

Eventually come to a large dutch barn where the road forks (Grid ref: 542632). Keep left towards a group of houses at Upper Austin Lodge, then break away to the right just beyond the dutch barn on a path signposted to Shoreham. Cross a surfaced drive (leading to the golf clubhouse) and continue ahead following a farm track. Through a gateway enter a second field, and at the far side come to the golf course. Turn right along the right-hand hedgerow, then enter woods. The path now slants left along the hillside among trees, and climbs steeply up the slope.

Emerge near the head of the slope, cross a stile and cut half-left over the highest part of a large field to reach the corner of a woodland. This is part of a firing range (see Walk 4). Should a red flag be flying from a nearby flagpole, proceed no further until a sentry gives the go-ahead. The path enters the woods, crosses a track and continues among trees until coming alongside a field on the left. Cross another vague track with a scene of woodland devastation (caused by the 1987 storm), and follow the continuing path veering right towards the edge of the downs, there to find another flagpole marking the end of the danger area. Now the path steeply descends the western flank of the downs. The Darent gap is seen ahead opening to the Holmesdale valley, while the Darent stream itself glints far below.

Near the foot of the slope cross a driveway with a house on the left, cut along the lower edge of its garden and then through a patch of woodland scrub. Come to a field and cross half-left to a stile giving onto the A225 (Grid ref: 526619). Bear left for about 30 yards, then turn right along a tree-enclosed footpath and cross the railway line. Walk ahead on the left-hand edge of a large field and reach a crossing track. Turn left and follow the field boundary to Shoreham churchyard. Here a gate on the right gives access to the churchyard; walk through it along a yew-lined path.

Leave the churchyard at the lych gate and walk along a street until reaching a hump-backed bridge over the Darent in the heart of Shoreham (3). Turn right just before the bridge. (For a note of interest, just over the bridge The Kings Arms has a novel "ostler's box" where in the pre-motor age a man would wait until required to look after a customer's horse. The box is inhabited today by a dummy ostler.)

Back on the walk bear left in front of The Water House (4) and follow a footpath alongside the Darent stream. On coming to a footbridge cross to the left bank and continue to follow the Darent. (The route is waymarked Darent Valley Path.) Eventually cross a stile into a large field; then over a second field, on the far side of which the way crosses a farm road and soon comes to a hop garden. Wander along the left-hand side of this and at last emerge by some farm-workers' houses on a lane. Walk ahead along this lane, passing Castle Farm on the right with its miniature windmill down by the stream; and soon arrive back at the Lullingstone Park Visitor Centre.

Items of interest:

1: Lullingstone Castle. Not a traditional fortified castle, but a Tudor manor house with a Queen Anne façade. Sir John Peche built the original manor house in the reign of Henry VIII, who was a frequent visitor. There is a castellated brick gatehouse and, within the grounds, the tiny Norman church of St Botolph with flint-studded walls and a collection of memorials to generations of Castle residents. Lullingstone Castle is open to the public on set days between Easter and October.

2: Lullingstone Roman Villa. Often described as the most exciting archaeological discovery in post-war Britain, the remains of a Roman nobleman's villa include beautiful mosaic tiled floors and evidence of an early Christian chapel. Now in the care of English Heritage, the villa is open daily to the public between early April and the end of September.

3: Shoreham. One of the most attractive of villages in the Darent valley, it has a number of lovely tile-hung or flint walled cottages, several pubs (one still with an ostler's box), a fine church and a picturesque bridge over the stream. There is a war memorial by the bridge, but on the slope of the downs above the village to the west a large cross has been cut in the chalk as additional testament to local men who died in two world wars. The village has connections with John Wesley, who came regularly for forty years to preach here, and also with William Blake and Samuel Palmer (see note 4). Edward Calvert, a friend of Palmer's, once wrote of the Darent valley near Shoreham as being "so hidden from the world that the devil has not yet found it".

4: The Water House. In this Queen Anne house the painter and poet Samuel Palmer (1805-1881 - not 1884 as the plaque on the house suggests) lived and worked for a period of seven years. He was much inspired by the valley and whilst at Shoreham produced some of his finest landscapes. Palmer greatly admired William Blake, who visited him here.

WALK 6: STANSTED - FAIRSEAT - HODSOLL STREET - RIDLEY - STANSTED

Distance:	5¹/₂ miles
Maps:	OS Pathfinder TQ 66/76 Chatham 1:25,000
	OS Landranger 188 Maidstone & The Weald of Kent 1:50,000
Start:	The Black Horse, Stansted (Grid ref: 606621)
Access:	By minor road (Vigo Road) running north-west of the A227 from a crossroads about 3¹/₂ miles south of Meopham.
Parking:	Near The Black Horse pub.
Refreshments:	Pubs in Stansted and Hodsoll Street.

Gentle vales scooped from the heart of the downs provide landscape features that lead the eye to distant views where dark woodlands balance bright slopes of wheat, rape or meadows grazed by cattle and horses. Isolated farms with the weight of centuries in their beams add architectural romance, and three small villages (in addition to Stansted) provide a sense of community in a truly rural scene. The best is Hodsoll Street; neat cottages and a pub grouped around a triangular green. Fairseat has a tiny church and a duckpond opposite; Ridley's church is almost absorbed by a neighbouring farmyard, with an attractive thatched well-head nearby.

* * *

From The Black Horse walk uphill along Tumblefield Road for about 200 yards, then turn left on a footpath by a small car park reserved for the residents of nearby houses. A stile gives access to a field, and another leads out of it on the far side to descend among scrub to a third stile. Bear half-right and follow a line of posts to the foot of a slope in a pleasant inner valley caught among rucks of downland. Now rise to the top far corner and enter Mingram Wood. A clear path winds through, then along a narrow woodland shaw before emerging just short of the timber-framed Coldharbour (Grid ref: 610612).

Head to the left towards Coldharbour's boundary fence, and over a stile cross a small field to its lower right-hand corner and another stile. Now descend directly ahead to a stile in the bottom

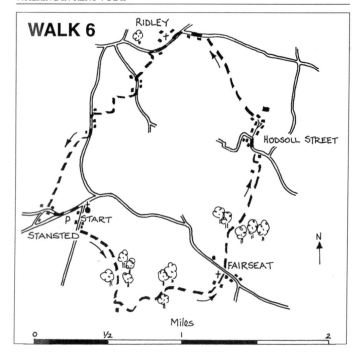

boundary, beyond which the way heads left along the bed of a narrow valley. Near the end of this valley-bed field veer right up the slope to enter the south-western corner of Wessell's Wood. Continue uphill. Near the top of the slope bear left on a footpath winding through the upper woodland edge, then veer left on a steady descent among a tangle of scrub and trees. Reach a sloping field; go down the left headland, and when the boundary cuts to the left, break away directly across the field to a pair of stiles in the lower boundary.

Now rise over three fields linked by stiles and field gates (fine views back to Stansted church) before bearing left on the hilltop towards Court House Farm. A track, then drive, leads through the farmyard and out to Vigo Road beside the small church of Fairseat (Grid ref: 622615). Cross to a swing-gate left of a duckpond, enter a

Bowdler's Well at Ridley (dated 1810) has a novel thatched roof

field and aim for its far left-hand corner. Over a stile walk across another field to a second stile among trees, then continue ahead towards the combined Westfield and Hall Woods. Enter these and immediately come to a crossing path. Take the right-hand branch through coppiced woodland. When the way forks take the left option and exit near a small pond.

Go ahead along the right-hand side of a long hedgerow (mostly holly) which leads to a bridleway funnelled between hedges, then out to a crossing track near farm buildings. Bear left into the farmyard and 25 yards later go right through a field gate and along a track to the small village of Hodsoll Street. Walk ahead along a road, and at a junction continue straight ahead, soon to reach an attractive village green by The Green Man pub. Continue, then bear left on a drive by Holywell Farm. Pass between a shingle-hung cottage and some barns, and enter a large field with a choice of paths. Walk across this open field to its lower right-hand corner and another field gate. Through the gate walk up the slope towards the left-hand boundary. Two-thirds of the way up the slope cross a stile on the left, then slant half-right over the highest part of the hilltop

45

field. (Extensive patchwork views from here.) Leave the field by way of a stile just to the right of farm buildings, and turn left on a lane called Bunker's Hill (Grid ref: 620639).

At a T junction bear left to the few buildings of Ridley. Note the handsome thatched Bowdler's Well (dating from 1810) near St Peter's church. The road slopes downhill. Pass a house on the left, and a short distance beyond it cut sharply back to the left on a bridleway. About 100 yards later break away to the right on a path descending to a stile. Ahead is a large open field. The path cuts through it, heading half-left towards the top corner near which a gap in the hedge gives access to a lane opposite Campbell's Cottage. Bear left up Haven Hill, rounding a bend at the top. Immediately after passing the driveway to a house on the right, take a fenced path which parallels the drive and then enters another large field.

Follow the right-hand boundary until it cuts back to the right. Now head left across the field to a stile in the opposite hedge. Cross this and walk downhill to a country lane joined through a field gate left of a bungalow (Grid ref: 608632). Bear left and soon pass the thatched, timber-framed Malt House. Baker's Wood is on the right of the lane. Just beyond it enter a field on the right and go half-left up a slope towards a crown of trees. Before reaching them veer leftwards on a line towards a tall radio mast (good views to the left). A series of stiles direct the way over several fenced paddocks, then out to a country road near some stables. Bear left, and left again at a junction, and wander back to Stansted church and The Black Horse.

WALK 7: TROSLEY COUNTRY PARK - COLDRUM STONES - TROSLEY

Distance:	3 miles
Maps:	OS Pathfinder TQ 66/76 Chatham 1:25,000
	OS Landranger 188 Maidstone & The Weald of Kent 1:50,000
Start:	Trosley Country Park (Grid ref: 635612)
Access:	Signposted from A227 Wrotham-Gravesend road near Vigo village.

Parking: Trosley Country Park - the gates are locked at dusk.
Refreshments: None on route.

Situated on the very lip of the North Downs Trosley Country Park consists largely of mixed woodland - beech, yew, oak, hornbeam and ash - which took a beating in the Great Storm of 16 October 1987. But the clearance of that storm has opened ever-wider views over the broad expanse of the Weald to complement those of the steep open meadows on the scarp slope. Within the Park there is plenty of car parking space (much needed at weekends and during school holidays), a picnic area, public toilets, Visitor Centre and a nature trail. Several circular walks are waymarked from the Park, and leaflets giving details are available from the Visitor Centre. This walk is a variation of one of them; a short walk with plenty of interest and fine views. It visits the church at Trottiscliffe (pronounced Trosley) and the Coldrum Long Barrow where our Neolithic forebears buried their dead some 4000 years ago.

*   *   *

From the Visitor Centre descend to a track (the North Downs Way) with views into the Weald below, and bear left. In 300 yards come to a waymarked path heading downhill. Descend a series of wood-braced steps leading to the foot of the tree-clad slope. At a crossing

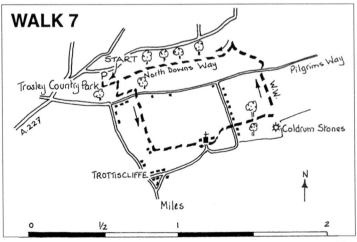

path turn left alongside a wire fence, and 300 yards later head to the right through wooden barriers, cross the narrow lane of the Pilgrims Way and enter a field where the view includes Trottiscliffe church. Walk down the edge of this field and a second, much-larger one. When the boundary of the second field cuts back to the right, continue straight ahead to the back of houses. Shortly after reach a crossing path and turn left (Grid ref: 642604).

The way now leads between fields and comes directly to the farmyard of Trosley Court. Pass in front of Trottiscliffe church (1). Next door to it is the eighteenth-century stone cottage called Whitakers. Immediately past this a path rises on the left, affording good views back onto the church. The path goes between fields to Pinesfield Lane and a row of bungalows. Cross the lane and walk directly ahead on a track; it leads through trees and narrows to a footpath across a field enjoying views of the North Downs. On the far side of the field come to a crossing path and bear right. About 150 yards later the Coldrum Stones (2) will be found to the right of a concrete farm road (Grid ref: 654607).

For the continuing walk return towards the North Downs, and maintain direction on the path of the Wealdway which initially goes between hedges, then along the left-hand side of a large open field, to reach the Pilgrims Way once more. Bear right, and a few paces later go left on the North Downs Way; a footpath which slants up the face of the downs in the shade of yew tees, then steepens towards the top. Gain the head of the slope and break away sharply left on the continuing North Downs Way among woods. This same path leads all the way back to the car park and Visitor Centre of Trosley Country Park.

Items of interest:

1: Trottiscliffe Church. Dedicated to St Peter and St Paul, this Norman church is delightfully set among farm buildings some distance from the village it serves. With its flint-studded tower and sarsen stones in its foundations, the church was built by William the Conqueror's Bishop Gundulph in 1100 on the site of a Saxon place of worship pulled down by the Normans. The fine pulpit came from Westminster Abbey.

2: The Coldrum Stones (See p18). The remains of a Neolithic burial chamber built some 4000-5000 years ago. The massive sarsen stones originally stood in a circle measuring about 160ft in circumference, and represent just one of several sites of the Medway Culture. Skeletal bones of 22 people and assorted animals were discovered when the chamber was excavated.

WALK 8: CAMER COUNTRY PARK - LUDDESDOWN - GREAT BUCKLAND - CAMER PARK

Distance:	6 miles
Maps:	OS Pathfinder TQ 66/76 Chatham 1:25,000
	OS Landranger 177 East London Area 1:50,000
Start:	Camer Country Park (Grid ref: 650669)
Access:	Via B2009 north-east of Meopham. Park entrance off Camer Park Road. Nearest station: Sole Street.
Parking:	Camer Country Park.
Refreshments:	None on route, but pubs at Lower Luddesdown and Meopham (both about 400yds from the path).

It seems hard to believe that Camer Country Park is less than 4¹/2 miles from the heart of Gravesend as the crow flies, and Luddesdown a similar distance from Rochester, for this walk leads through some delightful, peaceful countryside divorced from the world of commerce and industry in all save the distant march of electricity pylons. It's a popular walk based in part on one of the circular routes publicised in a Country Park booklet, and is waymarked as such. The Park, where it begins, is owned and managed by Gravesham Borough Council.

* * *

From the Country Park (1) entrance off Camer Park Road, walk directly ahead (public toilets to the right) along the parkland edge, soon with the handsome eighteenth-century Camer Court seen on the left. Leave the Park at the far left-hand corner by a lodge beside the B2009, then turn sharp right on a track running alongside the Park's boundary. This is the route of the Wealdway (2). Remain on the track as it veers left away from the Park and follow it beyond a

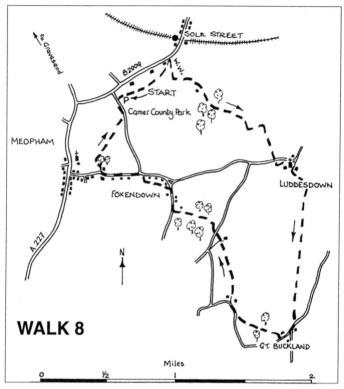

WALK 8

solitary house to the edge of Henley Wood where it forks. Continue along the left-hand edge of the wood, then go through a gap in a hedge and walk along the side of a field towards a pylon. Beyond this go through a narrow strip of woodland, then bear right in a field on Henley Down with Luddesdown church seen in the valley. Cross a stile and descend through scrub, then bear left along the top edge of a sloping field for about 200 yards before turning right and descending on a footpath. At the foot of the slope rise among trees to a narrow lane (Grid ref: 667663).

Cross over and climb some steps to a field. Walk directly ahead to reach a fence which forms the boundary to Luddesdown Court

(3). Bear left and in the field corner cross a stile, descend to a junction of minor roads and turn right by Luddesdown church (4). A private road goes ahead to Luddesdown Court, with a choice of paths by the gateway. Take the route along the drive, passing a large fanciful house on the left and the church on the right. Just before the drive ends at a farmyard cross a stile on the left and follow the path which scores a straight line alongside a fence then hedgerow, and rises uphill to gain very fine views back onto Luddesdown. (Enjoy this peaceful countryside and reflect that in the 1970s the Ministry of Defence planned to use it as a tank training ground!)

Near the head of the slope veer slightly right to cross a stile and continue on the upper edge of a field above a valley known as the Bowling Alley. When the boundary cuts back to the right towards a woodland, continue directly ahead across the field to a stile, and along the left-hand edge of a second field. A short distance along the fence cross another stile and maintain direction through the next two fields. At the far side come onto a narrow road and turn right, and when it forks after a few paces take the right-hand branch towards Great Buckland Farm (Grid ref: 669642).

A few paces beyond the farm go up some steps and into a field. Cross two stiles and head up the slope towards the woodland crown of Rochester Forest. Ascend a flight of wooden steps through the wood, and then walk half-left up a hilltop field, over a stile in a fence and across to the far right-hand corner of a second field to join a narrow lane. Bear right and soon come to Coomb Hill Farm, a lovely half-timbered fifteenth-century farmhouse with a large barn nearby. Continue ahead between the farmhouse and the barn on a track that narrows to a footpath along the edge of Dilmer Wood. Beyond the wood the path slopes down among thorn scrub and comes to a driveway near Dene Manor. Cross the drive and then wind up a slope among trees to reach a very narrow lane (Dene Road).

Cross to a track which soon provides views to Luddesdown again. At the top of a slope join a stony track and continue ahead through Brimstone Wood and on to another narrow lane. Turn right, and after about 300 yards bear left on a footpath among trees and alongside a fence at the bottom of a row of gardens. Eventually rejoin Foxendown Lane, bear left and continue for about 500 yards. The lane makes a right-hand bend by Foxendown Farm. Immediately past a white house on the right take a narrow footpath into woods and, before leaving the trees, head to the right on a clear path. Leaving the woods bear right to a field corner, walk along the left-hand boundary a few paces, then through a gap in the hedge and take the path heading diagonally across a large field. This leads to Camer Park Road. Bear left to gain the entrance to the Country Park.

Items of interest:

1: Camer Country Park. Established in 1971 it comprises some 45 acres of parkland. The Park closes at dusk.

2: The Wealdway. A long-distance footpath totalling 82 miles, which begins beside the Thames at Gravesend and finishes at Beachy Head overlooking the Channel.

3: Luddesdown Court. This handsome Grade I manor is said to have once been owned by Bishop Odo (half-brother of William the Conqueror) and is one of the oldest continuously occupied houses in Britain.

4: Luddesdown Church. Dedicated to St Peter and St Paul it was mentioned in the Domesday Book, but was largely rebuilt in 1866. The tower is fourteenth-century, as is the south porch.

WALK 9: HIGH HALSTOW - HALSTOW MARSHES - ST MARY HOO - HIGH HALSTOW

Distance:	7 miles
Maps:	OS Pathfinder TQ 67/77 Gravesend & Tilbury and TQ 87 Isle of Grain 1:25,000
	OS Landranger 178 Thames Estuary 1:50,000
Start:	Northward Hill Reserve, High Halstow (Grid ref: 782757)
Access:	Via Northward Avenue, signposted from the main street in High Halstow.
Parking:	At entrance to the Reserve.
Refreshments:	None on route.

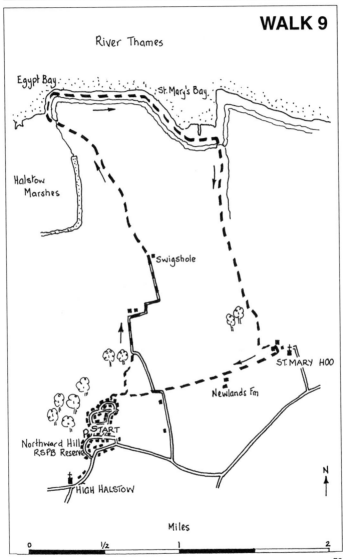

WALK 9

River Thames

Egypt Bay

St. Mary's Bay

Halstow
Marshes

Swigshole

ST. MARY HOO

Newlands Fm

START

Northward Hill
RSPB Reserve

HIGH HALSTOW

N

Miles

| 0 | ½ | 1 | 2 |

The RSPB's Northward Hill Reserve contains Britain's largest heronry. Although the walk does not actually enter this woodland, car parking is advised at its entrance, reached by way of Northward Avenue. In spring the woodland is extra lively with birdsong, and bluebells and violets make a lush carpet between the trees. Walkers are recommended to find time to wander its various footpaths either before or after completion of the described route, which heads north through arable farmland to marsh and estuary - a lonely, isolated patch of country - before returning inland to the hamlet of St Mary Hoo and back to High Halstow again. Anyone keen on birdwatching should carry binoculars, for the marshes and mudflats provide a rich habitat for numerous ducks, geese and waders.

* * *

From the car park walk back to Northward Avenue and turn left along it until reaching Longfield Avenue. Turn left again and at the end of the road take an enclosed footpath between houses into a hedge-bounded meadow. Walk along the right-hand boundary a few paces, then bear right over a stile to follow the path of the Saxon Shore Way (1). This footpath heads between open fields. On coming to a line of trees cutting left to separate two fields, turn left and walk alongside them until reaching the field corner. Bear right between trees, go over a stile and veer left down a slope with views emerging over the marshes to the Thames. Passing between bushes come to a narrow lane, Decoy Hill Road (Grid ref 786765).

Walk downhill along the lane, passing first Decoy Farm, and then the last house, Swigshole. Beyond this the lane becomes a track projecting roughly northward through a low-lying, crouching, windblown land of shaking reeds and watery channels. About ³/₄ mile beyond Swigshole the track forks. Ignore the right-hand concrete option and continue ahead, soon coming to a gateway where the track curves leftwards. Now leave the track and go up onto a grass-covered embankment ahead, on the edge of Egypt Bay. Across the Thames can be seen oil refineries at Coryton and Canvey Island, but immediately below, when the tide has receded, exposed mudflats are busy with birdlife.

Bear right and wander along the sea wall embankment for about 1¹/₂ miles. On the right an extensive region of flat land is often crowded with ducks and geese, while waders and gulls stalk the estuarine margins. The wooded crown of High Halstow (207ft) is the loftiest piece of land in view.

Come to St Mary's Bay and curve round it. When the embankment swings sharp left (Grid ref: 796787) towards West Point, break away to the right on a path heading inland along the right-hand side of a drainage channel; large hedgeless fields stretch on either side. Come to the end of the channel and a crossing track. Continue in the same direction through a gate to follow a tractor trail across to another gate on the far side of a field. Enter rising land and walk uphill towards a group of trees; pass along their left-hand side and come to a farm track. Bear left and follow this through a farmyard near the handsome grey stone church of St Mary Hoo, now a private residence.

Before reaching the church turn sharp right along a track to pass some houses, then continue through fields towards Newlands Farm. Pass to the right of the farm and go ahead (ignoring a metalled drive on the left). Heading through large open fields come to a four-way path junction and continue ahead. Arrive soon after on a narrow lane just to the north of Clinchstreet Farm. Walk along the lane for almost 100 yards, then break away to the left on the route of the Saxon Shore Way, leading back to High Halstow.

On entering the hedge-enclosed meadow near houses, there is a choice of route to consider. The most straightforward is to bear left and go between houses to emerge in Longfield Avenue once more, then follow the outward route back to the car park. But an alternative is to proceed round the boundary of the meadow to the far left-hand corner. There enter the Northward Hill Reserve and follow a woodland footpath, bearing left at junctions, finally rising up some steps to emerge at the car park.

Items of interest:

1: The Saxon Shore Way. This long-distance route of 140 miles traces the old shoreline of Kent as far as possible from Gravesend to Rye in Sussex, passing numerous fortifications built to defend the county against the raiding Saxons.

GREENSAND HILLS AND
THE VALLEYS OF EDEN AND MEDWAY

Flowing east from Westerham the Holmesdale valley makes an effective divide between the chalk of the North Downs and the narrow wooded strip of the Greensand Ridge. The valley has a flat bed to it so the Darent which eases through finds it difficult to express vitality, and its progress to the Thames is generally sluggish - except when in flood.

South of the greensand hills the progress of the River Eden towards its confluence with the Medway at Penshurst is similarly checked by the constrictions of its flat bed, but when heavy rains cause flooding there is mischief abroad and the heavy clay of its valley does nothing to ease the problems suffered by villages and farms set on its banks.

The Darent rises on the northern slope of Crockham Hill just inside the county border, among rhododendrons and broad sweeps of bluebells. A few hundred yards away, on the southern slope of this same greensand hill, a tributary of the Eden - and thus the Medway - bubbles from a spring in a wildly romantic garden with one of the finest views of southern England spread below.

Almost everywhere along this chain of hills magnificent views are the just reward of those who wander its footpaths. And there are footpaths in plenty too. Not only the seductive waymarked trail of the Greensand Way, but miles and miles of linking paths that seem especially designed to bring the explorer to a dream-like display of beauty: far-off to the south a minor ridge hints of Sussex, deep below a glint of sunlight on water tells of a lake or a farm reservoir, maybe the steeple of a village church flashes its weathervane above a screen of trees, or a moulded coombe directs one's gaze to the handsome farm built by a Kentish yeoman several hundred years ago. Without doubt there will be an oast house or two adding that very special architectural signature to the landscape. A landscape to absorb.

Along the Greensand Ridge, and nestling on its slopes, a succession of villages lead to the market town of Sevenoaks: Crockham Hill, French Street, Toys Hill, Ide Hill, Sevenoaks Weald; each one with footpaths of appeal, each one linked by trails as old as the villages themselves. Or, in some cases, even older. Sevenoaks itself is crowned with the glory of Knole House and its extensive deer park. Knole looks to the North Downs, but it's only a short step to regain the splendour of the south where the Greensand Ridge plunges out of trees to the green lapping meadows of the Weald.

Keep heading east and you'll come to Ightham Mote, a medieval moated manor house, an elegant pile of stone and timber cradled by the hills. Escape to the south a little and there sits Shipbourne like a spider in a web of footpaths; a great place from which to explore this benevolent land.

Back among the greensand hills Plaxtol is a cascade of houses down a slope from the church with the little River Bourne sidling through meadows on its way to the Medway. Orchards and hop gardens lace the hills, and on the edge of West Peckham sunny fields have been given over to soft fruit. Here the greensand hills offer yet more extensive views. From the long-deserted church of East Peckham - deserted because the village moved away - all the world, it seems, is a billowing mass of blossom when the orchards below are clad with spring. East Peckham now denies itself those views, and instead looks to the Medway where Kent's major river has broken through this barrier of ancient ragstone.

Back to the valley of the Eden.

Only a comparatively small area, the Eden's valley is nevertheless rich in history and extravagant in its houses. Iron Age Man created hilltop encampments overlooking the valley. The legions of Rome stamped out a roadway through from north to south, and in Tudor times trumpets sounded a royal fanfare across the peaceful acres, while poets and princes alike gathered in the Great Hall of Penshurst, or wandered the grounds of Hever with a hawk upon their wrist.

Where they roamed, so may we. For the valley has a grid of footpaths, bridleways and green lanes. We may divert from these pathways to visit Hever Castle or Penshurst Place; we may follow footpaths into the Elizabethan street of Chiddingstone - owned by the National Trust - or sit on a low hill and dream away the hours while birds trill gently overhead. Or for the moderately energetic, there's always the Eden Valley Walk to consider; 14 miles from Edenbridge to Tonbridge.

Tonbridge is graced by the remains of its castle, built to protect an important crossing of the Medway. That river is easily crossed today by numerous bridges, and motorists will barely notice the peaceful quality of the waterway as they thunder overhead. Yet the Medway is well worth exploring. It may not be a great river, as rivers go. It may not have the bravura of a mountain torrent. It has no falls, no white-water rapids, no immediate charisma. But it does have a quiet charm that grows and grows with every renewed acquaintance. And it has the ability to entice the wanderer into the very heartland of Kent along a towpath journey with an eloquence all its own. At the time of writing Kent County Council is preparing an interpretive book devoted to the Medway as it journeys between Tonbridge and Rochester. Each one of its miles is an education and an opportunity for enjoyment of Kent's cherished heartland.

*   *   *

GREENSAND HILLS AND MEDWAY VALLEY COUNTRY PARKS AND OPEN SPACES:

1:   Toys Hill: 450 acres of woodland overlooking the Weald. Since the 1987 hurricane-force winds ripped through these woods, views have been opened considerably. About 2¹/₂ miles south of Brasted. (See Walk 13)

2:   Ide Hill: Another wood-crowned ridge with big views. About 32 acres on the southern side of Ide Hill village. Ide Hill stands just west of B2042, about 3 miles south of Riverhead off A25. (See Walks 14 & 15)

3:   Hanging Bank, Ide Hill: East of the village, 97 acres of woodland on the very lip of the Greensand Ridge. Superb views. (See Walks 14 & 15)

4:   Dryhill Picnic Park: Situated 1¹/₂ miles west of Sevenoaks, 22 acres of former ragstone quarry, now woodland and meadow with picnic tables and seats. Reached by signposted minor road off A25.

5:   Knole Park, Sevenoaks: A magnificent deer park extending to 1000 acres. Pedestrians only, although vehicle access is allowed for visitors to Knole House (NT). (See Walk 10)

6:   One Tree Hill: 34 acres of woodland on the crest of the hills about 2 miles south-east of Sevenoaks. (See Walk 20)

7:   Haysden Country Park: Lakes, parkland and woods covering 160 acres on the borders of the Medway west of Tonbridge. Much of the site has access for the disabled. (See Walk 16)

8:   Dene Park, Shipbourne: 220 acres of mixed woodland with forest walk and a picnic site.

9:   Manor Park Country Park: Situated on the southern edge of West Malling, 52 acres of parkland with a pleasant lake.

10:   Teston Bridge Picnic Site: On the left bank of the Medway, 32 acres of water meadows; riverside walks. (See Walk 22)

WALK 10: THE GREENSAND WAY (WEST KENT SECTION: CROCKHAM HILL - YALDING)

Distance:	21 miles
Maps:	OS Pathfinder TQ 45/55 Sevenoaks & Westerham and TQ 65/75 Maidstone 1:25,000
	OS Landranger 187 Dorking, Reigate & Crawley and 188 Maidstone & The Weald of Kent 1:50,000
Guidebook:	*Greensand Way in Kent* by Bea Cowan (KCC 1992)
Start:	Goodley Stock Road, Crockham Hill (Grid ref: 438521)
Finish:	Yalding Station (Grid ref: 685503)
Public transport:	Sevenoaks (2 miles off-route from Knole Park) and Yalding are both served by British Rail. Also some intermediate bus routes.
Refreshments:	Pubs at Toys Hill, Ide Hill, Shipbourne, Dunk's Green, West Peckham and Nettlestead Green.

The Greensand Way is already 50 miles old when it crosses the Surrey/ Kent border on Crockham Hill, near Westerham, and there are another 55 miles to go before it converges with the Saxon Shore Way at Hamstreet, south of Ashford. It's a truly scenic walk, one of the best of all long routes in Southern England, and the 21 mile stage through West Kent is mentioned here as an enticement to all who enjoy exercise in a sparkling series of landscapes. Most users of this book would no doubt shrink at the thought of tackling a 21 mile walk in one outing, but because of the number of small villages along the way where cars could be parked, it's quite feasible to nibble at the route in stages of 5 or 6 miles at a time. Waymarking is exemplary, and armed with the KCC guidebook mentioned above (and the necessary maps to give an overall view), few should have difficulty finding the way. The following route description therefore provides only brief outline notes.

* * *

A link route of 1¹/₂ miles feeds the start from Westerham. Otherwise it's possible to park cars on Crockham Hill Common (approached by a drive cutting east from the B269 a little downhill from Kent

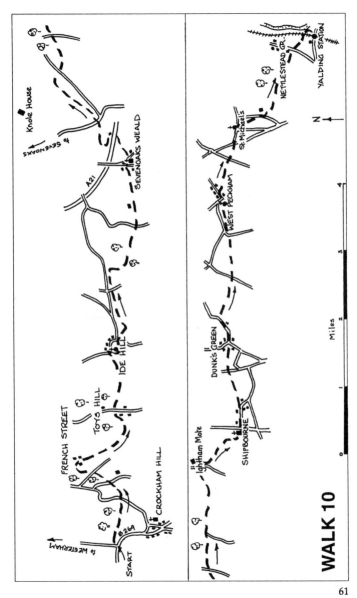

WALK 10

Knole House

to SEVENOAKS

A21

SEVENOAKS WEALD

FRENCH STREET

TOYS HILL

IDE HILL

to WESTERHAM

B269

START

CROCKHAM HILL

Ightham Mote

SHIPBOURNE

DUNK'S GREEN

WEST PECKHAM

St. Michaels

NETTLESTEAD GR.

YALDING STATION

N

Miles

0   1   2   3   4

Dale Farm at Sevenoaks Weald, (Walks 10 & 15)

Hatch). The waymarked footpath crosses the Common in two sections, then goes along the edge of Chartwell car park to French Street, a small secluded hamlet with a lovely valley leading to the National Trust woodland of Toys Hill. On this first section views have been partially concealed by trees, but on the way to Ide Hill the Weald is glimpsed on a number of occasions. Ide Hill (5 miles) is one of Kent's highest villages and a good walking centre. (See Walk 14.)

Continuing roughly eastward the very edge of the Greensand Ridge is followed for a while before dropping down the slope and across meadowland to Sevenoaks Weald. (Much of this section forms part of Walk 15.) Beyond Weald the footpath tunnels beneath the A21 and a mile further on enters the deer park of Knole Park (10 miles) on the outskirts of Sevenoaks. If the plan is to finish a stage here, Knole Park and Knole House (NT) are both worth exploring.

From Knole Park a brief woodland stretch returns the waymarked route once more to the very edge of the hills with more superb broad views over the Weald. From here to Ightham Mote another circular walk described elsewhere (Walk 20) shares this footpath. Ightham Mote is only a few paces off the Greensand Way, and it's worth making a short diversion simply to gaze at the impressive timber and stone south face of this lovely building rising from a narrow moat. The Greensand Way actually heads down a country lane for a very short distance, then cuts through woods and round the edge of fields to reach Shipbourne church (14^{1}/$_{2}$ miles).

Shipbourne lies below the Greensand Ridge, and a low-country walk heads east to Dunk's Green before climbing through orchards and over meadows below Mereworth Woods, then on to the attractive village green at West Peckham, sharing for a short distance the same path used by the Wealdway. The two ways part company in West Peckham, and the Greensand Way soon visits the lonely deserted church of St Michael, formerly the Parish Church of East Peckham before the village moved away. The church enjoys a magnificent panorama over the massed orchards of the Medway valley, while the Greensand Way slopes downhill through them, passes Roydon Hall, a centre for transcendental meditation, and just over a mile later comes to the River Medway near Yalding Station.

WALK 11: WESTERHAM - FRENCH STREET - WESTERHAM

Distance:	5 miles
Maps:	OS Pathfinder TQ 45/55 Sevenoaks & Westerham 1:25,000
	OS Landranger 187 Dorking, Reigate & Crawley and 188 Maidstone & The Weald of Kent 1:50,000
Start:	Westerham green (Grid ref: 447540)
Access:	On the A25 about 5 miles west of Sevenoaks. Buses from Sevenoaks, Oxted and Bromley.
Parking:	Car park by A25 near Quebec House on east side of Westerham (Grid ref 449541).
Refreshments:	Pubs and cafes in Westerham. Cafe at Chartwell.

This circular walk is a real gem that explores some quiet little valleys, woodland, hilltop crests with big views, and wanders alongside Chartwell, one-time home of Sir Winston Churchill. It's a switchback of a route with several steep, though short, ascents and descents to tackle; a fine walk to enjoy in all seasons.

Leaving Westerham the path goes alongside trim gardens watered by the Darent

Begin on the triangular village green near Westerham (1) Parish Church. On the green is a bronze statue of Churchill by Oscar Nemon, while General James Wolfe holds his sword aloft nearby. Cross the A25 near the Churchill statue and walk ahead down Water Lane, a narrow alleyway that leads between walls, crosses two branches of the Darent stream alongside a neat garden, and enters the foot of a sloping meadow. Walk up the slope to find a stile in the skyline fence. Over this cut across the hilltop meadow slightly left to reach a squeeze stile by an oak tree. Continue along an enclosed footpath to reach the B2026. Cross with care and turn right. A short distance up the road come to a minor junction and bear left on a lane signposted to French Street (Grid ref: 453533).

After about 100 yards break away left along a track which descends towards a solitary house, then head to the right on a footpath. In a few paces pass near the entrance to Hosey Cave (barred to keep people out, whilst still enabling a colony of bats to fly to and fro). The path winds up among woods and then forks. Continue straight ahead, now out of the woods but going along a tunnel of trees. Come to Gillhams Farm and turn left on a drive

Chartwell, former home of Sir Winston Churchill, now in the care of the National Trust *(Walk 12)*
The moat at Groombridge Place *(Walk 19)*

Igtham Mote, one of the finest of all medieval manor houses, now in the care of the National Trust *(Walk 20)*

This track through Mereworth Woods is also shared by the Wealdway *(Walk 21)*

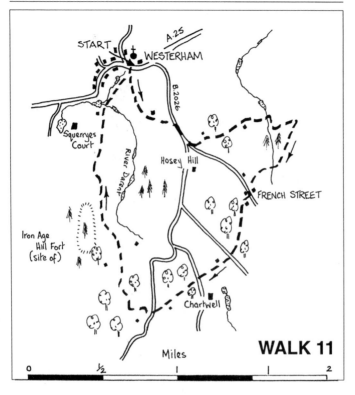

WALK 11

towards stables, then head right to pass through a gate where the path forks. Take the right-hand option and descend (lovely views left) into woods. At the foot of the slope join a track, cross a stream and swing to the right. A footpath soon cuts off to the left. Follow this steeply uphill among gorse bushes. Almost on the brow of the hill come to crossing tracks and turn right on a high path overlooking the deep and narrow valley just crossed. It now slopes gently downhill again, then bears right to enter conifer woods.

Walk through the woods, cross a stream and emerge into a sloping field. Go up the left-hand edge to a stile in the top corner. A path now eases along the hillside and emerges onto a narrow lane in the hamlet of French Street. Bear left for a few paces, then right on a drive leading to a house called Mannings Wood. A bridleway goes ahead alongside the boundary hedge of the house and eventually comes to a very narrow surfaced drive. Turn sharp left onto a footpath (Greensand Way) which leads through storm-thinned woods and at last reaches yet another narrow lane. Ahead there are two paths. Take the left-hand option, in effect continuing straight ahead. Soon enclosed by fences it leads down a slope along the boundary of Chartwell (2) grounds, with views left over a series of small lakes, Churchill's house and a fine panorama of the Weald.

Come to a country road by the entrance to Chartwell car park, cross ahead and ascend a steep slope on timber-braced steps to a wooded common. At the top of the slope walk directly ahead (still on the Greensand Way), ignoring all alternative footpaths. The way leads among bilberries, bracken, heather and rhododendrons, with oak, pine and sweet chestnut trees providing shade. Cross a narrow driveway and come to a fence boundary. Bear right and soon descend a sunken track to the B2026 (Grid ref: 448515).

Cross slightly to the right and walk down the driveway of April Cottage; when it curves left into a gateway continue ahead, then bear left at a junction of paths. Rise up a slope onto Crockham Hill Common and come to another path junction. Leaving the Greensand Way bear right for about 160 yards, then head to the right at yet another path junction. This path is a delight as it eases downhill among silver birch and pine, becoming a tight little trail brushed with rampant rhododendrons as the descent steepens.

Emerge below the common to a view north along Squerryes Park. Cross a stile by a field gate and walk through gentle meadows, veering half-left to find another stile on the edge of woods. On the right will be seen the course of the infant Darent, which rises in a private garden at the foot of the common. The way continues alongside the woods (which disguise the site of an Iron Age hillfort), and eventually reaches a dirt track. Follow this as it winds uphill and then curves left. On the brow of the hill, with Squerryes Farm seen below, come to a junction of paths. Cross a stile on the right, walk through a wooded grove and continue ahead with views to the North Downs. The path soon plunges steeply downhill with Westerham seen strung out below, and comes to a track by Park

Lodge.

Walk down the track to a pond on the left. A concrete footbridge crosses the Darent on the right, with a footpath continuing from it along the bottom edge of a sloping meadow. Eventually reach another stile on the left. This leads to Westerham green along Water Lane where the walk began.

Items of interest:

1: Westerham. The first villagers built their huts within a stockade on what is now the green, but in 1227 Henry III granted a charter to allow a market here, thus giving Westerham the status of a town. There are several fine old buildings, including the 700-year-old Grasshopper above the green. James Wolfe was born at The Vicarage in 1727, but spent his childhood living at the red-brick, multi-gabled house now known as Quebec House after his famous victory in Canada. Quebec House is in the care of the National Trust and open to the public.

2: Chartwell. Home to Sir Winston Churchill from 1924 until his death in 1965, Chartwell (NT) stands on a high terrace of land overlooking a great sweep of gardens, parkland and lakes, with woods to east and west and a lovely view south into the Weald. The house is now very much a museum devoted to Churchill's long life and varied careers, but several rooms are kept as they were in his lifetime. The studio, containing many of his own paintings, is also open to the public.

WALK 12: CROCKHAM HILL - TOYS HILL - PUDDLEDOCK - CROCKHAM HILL

Distance:	5¹/₂ miles
Maps:	OS Pathfinder TQ 45/55 Sevenoaks & Westerham 1:25,000
	OS Landranger 187 Dorking, Reigate & Crawley and 188 Maidstone & The Weald of Kent 1:50,000
Start:	Holy Trinity Church, Crockham Hill (Grid ref: 444507)
Access:	On B2026 midway between Edenbridge and Westerham. The church stands 150 yards east of the main road.

Parking:	With discretion in the village.
Refreshments:	None on route.

This particular walk is just one of many that could be adopted in this western corner of the county where footpaths abound and broad views encompass scenes of great beauty. It's countryside that was known and loved by Octavia Hill, one of the co-founders of the National Trust, who walked these same footpaths and now lies buried in Crockham Hill churchyard. Much of this walk has Octavia Hill connections, either through the National Trust or from more personal association. At Toys Hill is a cottage in which she lived for a short time; in that same hilltop hamlet she sunk a well for the benefit of the villagers. Returning over Mariners Hill the walk passes close by a seat she erected in memory of her mother, on land that meant much to her. In fact she personally fought to save this magnificent hilltop crown for the nation, and actually received a cheque to finalise its purchase only the day before she died. As you walk this route, spare a moment to consider the effect her tremendous vision had on our ability to enjoy access to this countryside - and give thanks.

*   *   *

Begin near the Parish Church, where the approach road makes a left-hand bend by the village school. Directly ahead a swing gate next to a field gate gives access to a meadow at a dedicated picnic area. Cross this picnic area to a stile, then slant down to the bottom right-hand corner of the meadow and go onto a lane. Bear left along the lane for about 400 yards to its end at Acremead Cottage. A track heads left, while the driveway to Chandlers rises ahead a little to the right. Go up this drive and on coming to a gateway turn left and wander along an enclosed grass path through a garden, then swing right and descend past a vegetable plot with a huge view growing ahead. Enter a sloping meadow and go down to its bottom left-hand corner.

Pass through a field gate by a stream and rise on the far side heading half-right to the top right-hand corner. There another stile leads into a woodland shaw. The path goes through it and continues along the left-hand edge of the trees. At the end of the shaw bear right and over a stile enter a large field where a line of oak trees leads towards a small wood. Cut across to the right-hand corner of the

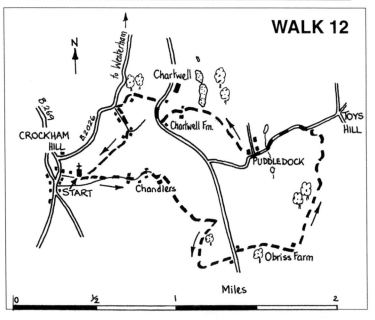

WALK 12

N

to Westerham

B 269

B 2026

Chartwell

CROCKHAM HILL

Chartwell Fm.

TOYS HILL

PUDDLEDOCK

START

Chandlers

Obriss Farm

Miles

0   ½   1   2

wood, then bear half-left to pass alongside a cattle trough. Continue across the brow of the field to the far side and come onto a farm track by way of another stile. Turn left along the track as far as a country road. Turn left again and a few paces later bear right by a cottage and walk along another track to Obriss Farm (Grid ref: 466501).

Pass to the right of the farmhouse and go through a field gate by a barn. Bear left along the edge of a large meadow. Come to another field gate with a stile and enter a second meadow. Cut across to the far right-hand corner, go through a line of trees and across a much smaller meadow to the end of a small woodland. Through the trees walk half-left ahead to find a stile in a fence. The continuing path is somewhat tangled for a few paces, but it soon improves to wind among trees, then broadens to a track that curves left to rise towards a private garden. Immediately before this garden turn right on a narrow footpath that leads to the drive of Bardogs Farmhouse at Toys Hill (Grid ref: 467512). In a few paces come to a narrow lane and bear left. (Octavia Hill's wellhead is found a short distance along the lane to the right.)

Descend the lane with caution (it has high banks and blind corners) for about ½ mile to a small group of cottages at Puddledock. Just beyond the last of these turn right to cross a stile by a field gate and walk ahead along a track that soon narrows to a path leading to Chartwell Farm. Churchill's former home, Chartwell, can be seen ahead to the right (see Walk 11). Enter Chartwell Farmyard through a swing gate near an oast house, and walk up the drive which is full of colour in spring with a blaze of rhododendrons and azaleas. At the head of the drive (more lovely views left) turn right and walk along another country road (caution advised) for about 200 yards, then bear left onto a bridleway among trees.

Ignore alternative paths and maintain direction uphill. Near the head of the slope look for a field gate on the left which gives stunning views into the Weald. Do not go through the gate but continue along the path and cross a gravel drive (an isolated cottage is seen on the left). Follow a boundary fence ahead, and when the path forks bear left and come to the corner of a field. Turn right and

Froghole Farm is perched on a steep slope of hillside above Crockham Hill

walk along a footpath that leads directly to a flight of stone steps descending to the junction of a lane and the B2026. Before descending the steps a diversion to the left is worth taking; a footpath leads among trees and soon arrives at the stone seat erected by Octavia Hill in memory of her mother. (Beautiful views to the west.) Behind the seat the path crosses a stile and goes onto the brow of Mariners Hill and a wooden seat in memory of Octavia's friend and companion, Harriott Yorke, first treasurer of the National Trust. This seat enjoys a vast panorama to the south and east.

Return to the walk, descend the steps and go left along Froghole Lane. When the lane bends sharp left round a converted oast house (once owned by Octavia Hill), leave it for a footpath signposted to Crockham Hill Church that descends 134 stone steps, first past Spark Haw, then the thatched Buttles Steps Cottage. At the foot of the steps go down the edge of a field to a stream. Cross by a footbridge, and walk up the next undulating meadow (reshaped by a landslip in 1596) to Crockham Hill Church.

WALK 13: TOYS HILL - BRASTED - TOYS HILL

Distance:	6 miles
Maps:	OS Pathfinder TQ 45/55 Sevenoaks & Westerham 1:25,000
	OS Landranger 188 Maidstone & The Weald of Kent 1:50,000
Start:	National Trust car park, Toys Hill (Grid ref: 470516)
Access:	Head south off A25 on minor road signposted in Brasted.
Refreshments:	Pubs and cafe in Brasted, pub on Toys Hill.

Little more than a hamlet perched on the southern slope of the Greensand Ridge, Toys Hill boasted one of the finest beech-crowned sections of that ridge - until the Great Storm of October 1987. That night hundreds of acres of exposed National Trust woodland were flattened by the winds. In their place fresh views have opened onto the Weald, and now that most of the storm-damaged trees have been cleared away and thousands of replacement trees planted, footpaths once again entice across that lofty crown. This walk explores those woodlands (and others). In addition there are fine little valleys, country cottages and views of the North Downs, as well as the Weald. On the return from Brasted the route visits Emmetts garden (NT) which, like so many other places visited in this collection of walks, is particularly fine in bluebell time.

* * *

In the left-hand corner of the National Trust car park two paths begin by the side of a notice board; one climbs some steps, but ours, the right-hand option, begins by going straight ahead and very soon meets a broad crossing track. Turn left and follow this as it leads to an open grassy terrace with a commemorative stand of pine trees on the site of one-time Weardale Manor. About 100 yards beyond the track forks. Continue straight ahead, then gradually lose height with the North Downs seen far ahead. Ignoring alternatives the track winds downhill and leaves Toys Hill woodlands by the white-painted Highview Cottage (Grid ref: 464521).

A narrow metalled lane now leads ahead, gently dropping through a lovely valley. On reaching French Street Farm it winds uphill into the pretty hamlet of French Street (see Walk 11). Just after passing April Cottage cross a stile on the right. There are two footpath options and a view to the oasts of Outridge Farm. Take the left-hand path which skirts the top edge of a steep meadow (on the left a private burial ground), then slopes downhill, crossing two stiles. Over the second of these bear right to the foot of the slope, cross a stream and rise the other side through a woodland of conifers. Leaving the trees continue to rise uphill. At a 4-way junction of paths head to the right, go over a stile and across a hilltop meadow towards a tall timber-framed building. Reach this (Pipers Green) and bear left along a drive (Grid ref: 464534).

After the drive curves right to enter the grounds of Foxwold, continue straight ahead, now on an unsurfaced track that narrows to a path bordered by trees and rhododendrons. Eventually reach a country road, bear left and walk down it for $^1/_2$ mile to Brasted (1) and the A25.

Turn right in the village, and after about 100 yards or so turn right again into Elliotts Lane, at whose entrance is a white weatherboarded building. It's a short, narrow lane, and at its end a footpath cuts directly up the hillside to provide broad views. In

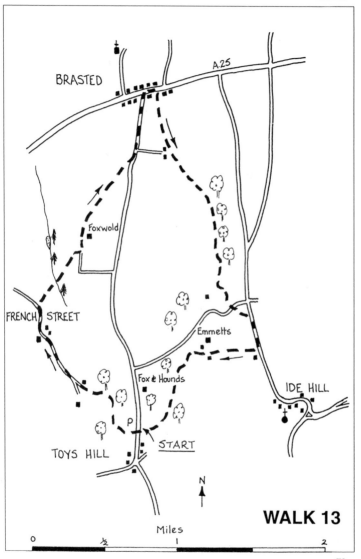

BRASTED

A.25

Foxwold

FRENCH STREET

Emmetts

Fox & Hounds

IDE HILL

P

START

TOYS HILL

N

WALK 13

Miles

0   ½   1   2

$^{1}/_{2}$ mile come to a track by some houses (Grid ref: 474544). Continue ahead, but when it curves right towards some dilapidated farm buildings, leave the track and take a footpath going ahead alongside a narrow belt of woodland, with fields on the right.

On meeting a junction of paths continue ahead rising uphill, now among trees. The path climbs through a gently-moulded valley. Just after passing a timber-framed building well off to the right, come onto a narrow country road. Bear right, and a few paces later, at the next bend, go left on another footpath which leads to a drive. Cross this, then over a stile into a large field. Ide Hill can be seen ahead, and Emmetts (a large grey National Trust property) to the right. The path crosses a corner of the field, aiming a little left of Ide Hill church, and comes onto a road (take care). Bear right and walk along it to reach Ide Hill Cricket Club's field and pavilion. Turn right and go up the long driveway leading to Emmetts.

Pass through gardens, keeping left of the house, with magnificent views over the Weald. The drive then veers sharp right in front of some low buildings (public toilets). Leave it here and walk ahead along the left-hand side of the buildings to join a path going uphill through rhododendrons into storm-damaged Scords Wood.

Turn left at cross-tracks. The way makes a right-hand curve and reaches more cross-tracks. Continue ahead, eventually coming to open views with Bough Beech Reservoir seen below in the Weald. At a 4-way junction of tracks bear right on a path that rises slightly through the spacious Octavia Hill Woods and eventually leads to the road directly opposite the car park at Toys Hill (2). The Fox and Hounds pub is a short walk off to the right.

Items of interest:

1: Brasted. Like so many villages astride the A25, most of Brasted's shops have been steadily taken over by the antiques trade. One of its best features is the small strip of village green backed by a row of Tudor cottages. The church has had a chequered history. All but the medieval tower was demolished and rebuilt in 1860, but this was damaged by a flying bomb in World War II, which destroyed the glass and cracked the chancel walls. In the 1980s part of the church was destroyed by fire, but restoration work has now been completed and services are again conducted there. In 1840 Napoleon

III, nephew of Bonaparte, lived for a while at Brasted Place and in the grounds there trained a handful of troops in readiness for his return to France.

2: Toys Hill. The hamlet owes much to Octavia Hill, co-founder of the National Trust. At one time she owned a cottage overlooking the Weald, and had a well sunk for the benefit of the local community who, until then, used to carry their water from the foot of the hill. The well has long been closed, but its neat cover makes an interesting foreground to a vast Wealden view (Grid ref: 468513). Much of the hill is owned by the National Trust, as is Outridge Farm whose oast houses are clearly seen across the valley from French Street. Until the 1970s two pubs served Toys Hill, but now only the Fox and Hounds (situated on top of the hill beside the road) remains in business.

WALK 14: IDE HILL - MANOR FARM - IDE HILL

Distance:	4³/₄ miles (A route) 5¹/₂ miles (B route)
Maps:	OS Pathfinder TQ 45/55 Sevenoaks & Westerham 1:25,000
	OS Landranger 188 Maidstone & The Weald of Kent 1:50,000
Start:	Ide Hill village green (Grid ref: 486518)
Access:	Via B2042 south of A25 at Riverhead, near Sevenoaks.
Parking:	Beside B2042 south-east of the village (Grid ref: 488517)
Refreshments:	Pubs at Ide Hill and Whitley Row.

Third of that trinity of villages on the Greensand Ridge west of Sevenoaks (the others being Toys Hill and Crockham Hill), Ide Hill is well-known to walkers for its generous array of footpaths and magnificent views. Most of the village is grouped together near the large sloping green. There's a small general stores and a pub, The Cock, said to date from the sixteenth century, and above the green the highest church in Kent. From a viewpoint behind the church all the Weald is spread out in perfection below. Yet again, as with Crockham Hill and Toys Hill, there is a memorial here to Octavia Hill.

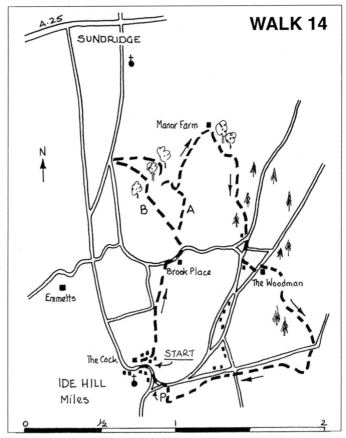

A small car park at a junction of roads behind the village hall has its own very special view south between projecting spurs to Bough Beech Reservoir glinting in the valley.

* * *

Facing The Cock from the village green note a narrow metalled road passing in front of the pub and running parallel with the main road. Walk along it and curve left to enter a small residential area, at the bottom of which a footpath goes between houses towards Brook

Place. Enter an open field with views ahead to the North Downs and left towards Toys Hill and the large grey house called Emmetts (see Walk 13). At the bottom of the field come onto a drive by The Ramblers and bear right. The footpath makes a dog's-leg curve round the edge of the garden before striking across more fields. Eventually reach a narrow country lane and turn right. This leads to Brook Place, seen off to the right (Grid ref: 491529).

By the entrance to Brook Place stands a black barn, and opposite (on the left), a track leads between houses and into a field where there are two footpaths.

Route A (the shorter option) slants right and rises across the field to a stile on the far side. A few paces beyond this come to a track and bear left. The track soon curves to the right and is joined by option B.

Route B goes straight ahead along the field boundary beside a stream with a small woodland on the left. Following the stream the path veers left and descends among trees, crosses the stream and rises again. Emerging from trees enter an enclosed field and walk ahead along its left-hand boundary. Near the top of the field cross into the adjacent hilltop field on the left, and walk across it heading half-right. Eventually reach a stile near a road (Grid ref: 484538). Do not leave the field; instead make a sharp right-hand elbow turn and cross to a gateway in the opposite hedge. Go through, bear right and follow the field boundary downhill. Near the foot of the slope head right among trees, steadily losing height through a very pleasant little vale, and come to a stream. Cross a footbridge, cut left and slant uphill to emerge from the woodland. Continue uphill near the right-hand edge of an area of bracken. On the brow of the hill come to a crossing track and turn left, joining Route A.

Routes A and B having combined, follow the track sloping downhill with the North Downs seen ahead broken by the Darent gap. The track forks. Continue ahead down the left-hand side of a line of pine trees. Cross a stile at the bottom and continue ahead towards isolated Manor Farm (Grid ref: 494542). At a crossing track near the farm turn right; it soon becomes a sunken track overhung with trees, magnificent with bluebells in spring. Wander through, then walk up the right-hand side of a coppice woodland. At the top join a track on the edge of conifer woods and bear right. Continue uphill and come to a definite 4-way crossing. Go straight ahead to reach a narrow country road by a house called Forest Edge (Grid ref: 497531).

Turn right and in a few paces come to a minor crossroads with a large triangle of grass. Continue ahead and immediately before reaching a white house (Beech Grove) bear left on a drive, then over a stile into a field. Across this come to another lane and head left.

Immediately after passing The Woodman bear right. There are two paths. Take the right-hand option, cross a stile and walk ahead across a field to find another stile on the far side. Over this go onto a track sloping downhill. Soon join a crossing track and bear right. This leads into Hyde Forest. Keep ahead through the forest rising uphill; when it opens with a field on the left another track breaks off to the right. Ignore this and continue ahead, now with coppice woodland on the right.

Come to a field gate. The path veers slightly right, weaves a pleasant course among conifers, then comes to another country road. Cross over and take a path half-right along the lip of the Greensand Ridge. The path forks. Take the left branch leading to a projection of ridge above the Weald (superb views). Head sharp right; the path winds above a steep drop, then parallels the road. Come to a Greensand Way marker and follow paths adopted by this route along the edge of the hillcrest towards Ide Hill. On coming to the B2042 again by Hanging Bank, cross to the car park, or finish at Ide Hill village green a little further up the road.

WALK 15: SEVENOAKS WEALD - BOARHILL - SEVENOAKS WEALD

Distance:	6 miles
Maps:	OS Pathfinder TQ 45/55 Sevenoaks & Westerham 1:50,000
	OS Landranger 188 Maidstone & The Weald of Kent 1:50,000
Start:	Sevenoaks Weald church (Grid ref: 529514)
Access:	By minor road signposted off A21 south of Sevenoaks.

| *Parking:* | In a lay-by just north of the church. |
| *Refreshments:* | None on route. |

Overlooking a broad panorama Sevenoaks Weald slumbers on the southern slope of the greensand hills. The Greensand Way passes across its northern edge, while other footpaths spread into the Weald to explore a patchwork of woods, fields and meadows. This walk does just that, taking advantage of a quiet agricultural landscape before climbing to the ridge and returning along the path of the Greensand Way. In winter, or after prolonged rain, some sections may be heavy with Wealden clay.

* * *

Immediately to the north of St George's church, Church Road meets Glebe Road. A few paces beyond this junction cross a stile on the left next to a field gate (Greensand Way marker). Go down the left-hand side of a field, through patches of gorse and over a brook, then up the slope to Dale Farm. Pass to the left of a converted oast house, bear right, then left by farm buildings and cross a field to a line of trees. Continue over the next field through a new plantation, and come to a stile among more trees. With large farm buildings seen

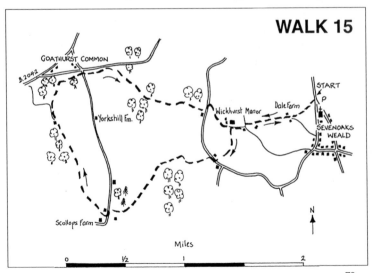

ahead, descend slightly left to cross a ditch, then rise on the other side to pass to the right of the buildings (Grid ref: 521512).

Go through a field gate near the barns, then aim half-left towards another line of trees. Wander down to a farm road, turn left and a few paces later bear right to pass Wickhurst Manor (1). Just before reaching the end of the farm drive go through a single gate on the left (thus leaving the Greensand Way) and walk across a field to its far corner where a stile is set among trees. Now follow the left-hand boundary of the field ahead to a second stile. Over this walk up a slope aiming slightly left of a house on the brow of the hill, and come to a country road. Turn right for about 40 yards, then cross a stile on the left. Straight ahead pass through a woodland shaw to a large field, which should be crossed aiming slightly right to meet the far boundary about 40 yards to the right of a wood (Grid ref: 512506).

Cross a stile and bear right along the headland of another field. The boundary swings left for a few paces, then breaks off to the right. At this point leave the headland and strike across the field to its bottom right-hand corner. There cross two stiles and go down the left-hand edge of a field to find another stile in the corner. The path forks. Take the right-hand option, in effect continuing straight ahead along a field boundary to the next corner. The way continues over a stile, then half-left alongside a fence to some trees. Through these cross an open field towards the left-hand corner of evergreen woods.

Walk alongside the woods, then over the top left-hand edge of a field, passing to the right of a farm. From the brow of the hill enjoy views of valley fields and the tree-scragged ridge above. At the bottom left-hand corner come onto a narrow country road opposite cottages. Bear left, and 30 yards later turn right through a field gate, then left across a small paddock beyond which the path enters a patch of woodland. Cross a stream by a footbridge and enter an open field (Grid ref: 499502).

Go straight across to a gap in the far boundary to face a hedgerow separating two fields. Walk along the left-hand side of the hedge, and at the far end cross a smaller field to a woodland shaw which opens to a large undulating field with Yorkshill Farm (2) seen half-right across it, with the Greensand Ridge above.

Cross half-left to a projection of trees, then wander up the headland to a narrow lane by a cottage (Boarhill on the map). Walk up the lane, but when it curves left take a footpath rising steeply up a slope of scrub. Come to a crossing track and go to the right. When it forks keep on the upper level with fine views overlooking Bough Beech Reservoir (3). The path soon rises among trees and reaches another crossing path. Bear right, now on the Greensand Way once more, and follow GW markers at all junctions.

The route traces the edge of the greensand hills, and at a parking area crosses half-left, over Yorks Hill Road, and onto the continuing Greensand Way. The path soon forks. Veer left, now walking parallel with a road. Eventually come to another fork where the GW branches right, and slope downhill with it among trees. Impressive views reveal Bough Beech Reservoir again. Cross a stile and go round the left-hand boundary of a field to another stile by a field gate in the opposite hedgerow. Now cross through the middle of an undulating meadow before veering right to enter an oak woodland (Harbour Hook).

The path winds through the woods and out to meadowland. Cross half-right towards Hatchlands Farm, passing alongside another woodland. Stiles direct the footpath round the left-hand side of the farm and onto a country road (Grid ref: 513513). Turn left, and 100 yards later cross a stile on the right. Walk down the edge of a large field, veering left when the hedge ends, and cross towards another farm. Rejoin the outward route near Wickhurst Manor to follow the Greensand Way back to Sevenoaks Weald (4).

Items of interest:

1: Wickhurst Manor. Although most of this manor house dates from the nineteenth century, it contains the original medieval hall. The outer wall has a stone doorway from the fifteenth century.

2: Yorkshill Farm. A fifteenth-century Wealden hall-house that looks most attractive from across the fields, and from the ridge above.

3: Bough Beech Reservoir. Created by the East Surrey Water Company by damming a valley feeding the River Eden, the reservoir was completed in 1969. Bayleaf, a handsome timbered farmhouse, was saved from the waters by being carefully dismantled and carted to the Weald and Downland Museum at Singleton (Sussex) and then reassembled. At the northern end of the reservoir a section has been set aside as a wildlife reserve. In a converted oast house at nearby Winkhurst Green, the Kent Trust for Nature Conservation has an information centre and a small but interesting museum to the hop industry.

4: Sevenoaks Weald. The heart of the village has a large and attractive green. To the south of it stands Long Barn, one-time home of Vita Sackville-West and Harold Nicolson, before they moved to Sissinghurst Castle where they created an outstanding garden. In 1936 the American aviator Charles Lindbergh bought Long Barn, and while there his wife Ann wrote *Listen, the Wind*. Sevenoaks Weald's literary association continues, as the village was also home for a while to that restless poet, Edward Thomas, who was killed in World War I, and in Thomas's cottage W.H.Davies wrote his *Autobiography of a Supertramp*.

WALK 16: THE EDEN VALLEY WALK
(EDENBRIDGE - HEVER - PENSHURST - TONBRIDGE)

Distance:	14 miles
Maps:	OS Pathfinder TQ 44/54 Tonbridge & Edenbridge 1:25,000
	OS Landranger 187 Dorking, Reigate & Crawley and 188 Maidstone & The Weald of Kent 1:50,000
Guidebook:	*Eden Valley Walk* by Caroline Wing (KCC 1991)
Start:	Edenbridge Parish Church (Grid ref: 445462)
Finish:	Tonbridge Castle (Grid ref: 589466)
Public transport:	Edenbridge and Tonbridge are linked by railway. Also several intermediate bus and rail links.
Refreshments:	Pubs in Hever, Penshurst and Tonbridge; cafes in Penshurst and Tonbridge.

One of a number of routes promoted by Kent County Council, the Eden Valley Walk was inaugurated in the spring of 1991. Where definitive footpaths allow, it traces the course of the rivers Eden and Medway through a low-lying valley between Edenbridge and Tonbridge, with the Greensand Ridge to the north and a High Wealden ridge to the south. In truth the walk begins a little west of Edenbridge to link the Vanguard Way (1) and the Wealdway (2), but it is more convenient to begin this particular linear route at the lychgate of the parish church. As the route is extremely well waymarked throughout, precise route descriptions are superfluous, but the guidebook mentioned above makes interesting reading and is highly recommended.

* * *

Initially the way leads through Edenbridge churchyard and a small residential estate, before crossing the Edenbridge-Uckfield railway line on a bridge, and entering fields. A succession of low-lying fields are then crossed until the route veers south to Delaware Farm, along the drive to Hever Road, then turns right for a few paces. A path goes across a small field towards a railway line, then under it by a brick archway. Soon join a lane leading to Lydens Farm, from which a field route crosses to another minor road near Hever Station (3 miles). A series of footpaths and country roads brings the route to the Henry VIII pub and Hever Parish Church (3).

From Hever churchyard an enclosed footpath gives views of a 35-acre lake in the grounds of Hever Castle (4). Eventually come to a group of houses, cross a quiet lane and take to fields again. The path enters coppice woodland and passes through a small sandstone gorge before coming to Hill Hoath. Beyond a farmyard both Chiddingstone Castle and Church can be seen off to the left (see Walk 17). The way now follows a grass track to another country road, crosses it and reaches the farm of Wat Stock. Far to the north the line of the greensand hills may be seen.

A mile-long farm track leads to Penshurst ($7^{1}/_{2}$ miles), crossing the River Eden shortly before reaching the B2176 opposite majestic Penshurst Place (5). Bear left on the road, then go over a stile into parkland and cut across to the church. Go through the churchyard and the original Leicester Square beyond, then beneath an archway to follow a drive alongside a wall enclosing the extensive gardens of Penshurst Place, with the young River Medway below to the right.

Go up a steep hillside to the left of Well Place Farm (views back to Penshurst are very fine), head along a concrete farm road and then by footpath to the banks of the Medway. Cross to the right bank at Ensfield Bridge, and soon enter scrub woodland along the cut of the Straight Mile, an incomplete section of the Medway's navigation. This leads directly to Haysden Water (6), now part of Haysden Country Park. Pass beneath the raised A21 and rejoin the Medway (and the route of the Wealdway) near the austere grey gates of the Flood Relief Barrier. The final 2 miles of the walk follow the Medway to Tonbridge Castle (7).

WALK 16

Items of interest:

1: The Vanguard Way. This little-known 62-mile walk links the suburbs of London with the Channel coast. From East Croydon to Seaford Head the route explores much surprisingly remote countryside. Guidebook: *The Wealdway & The Vanguard Way* by Kev Reynolds (Cicerone Press 1987)

2: The Wealdway. As its name suggests, this long-distance route crosses the Weald in its 82-mile journey from Gravesend on the banks of the Thames, to Beachy Head on the Sussex coast. A very fine walk. The guidebook is the same as that mentioned above which includes the Vanguard Way.

3: Hever Parish Church. Dedicated to St Peter, the church dates from the late thirteenth century, an attractive, slender-spired building that contains the tomb of Sir Thomas Bullen, father of the ill-fated Anne Boleyn.

4: Hever Castle. Inextricably linked with Henry VIII and a most turbulent period of English history, this birthplace of Anne Boleyn owes much of its present beauty and opulence to a wealthy American, William Waldorf Astor, who bought it in 1903 and then lavished a

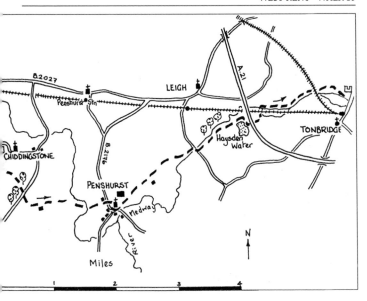

fortune on its restoration and improvement. The castle and gardens are open to the public and are well worth a visit.

5: Penshurst Place. One of the grandest of English stately homes, Penshurst Place is huge, yet Sir Philip Sidney, who was born there in 1554, described it as "handsome without curiosity and homely without loathsomeness". The original manor was built about 700 years ago, and the Great Hall at the heart of the building looks much as it did in the fourteenth century. The Place and its grounds are open to the public.

6: Haysden Water. A lake, created from gravel extraction works in the 1970s, has been adopted as part of the 165 acres of Haysden Country Park. Haysden Water is used for sailing and other water sports.

7: Tonbridge Castle. The remains of a stark Norman stronghold with drum towers built on a mound above the left bank of the Medway. To emphasize the strategic importance of the site, there has been some form of defensive fort here since Iron Age times.

One-time home of Anne Boleyn, Hever Castle is one of the gems on the Eden Valley Walk

WALK 17: CHIDDINGSTONE - PENSHURST PLACE - CHIDDINGSTONE

Distance:	6 miles
Maps:	OS Pathfinder TQ 44/54 Tonbridge & Edenbridge 1:25,000
	OS Landranger 188 Maidstone & The Weald of Kent 1:50,000
Start:	Chiddingstone Parish Church (Grid ref: 501452)
Access:	By minor road signposted off B2027 (Edenbridge-Tonbridge road). Chiddingstone is about 4 miles east of Edenbridge.
Parking:	With discretion in the village street.
Refreshments:	Pubs and tearooms in Chiddingstone and Penshurst.

Chiddingstone and Penshurst are two of the most interesting and attractive villages in all Kent; the first for the simple charm of its street of half-timbered houses, church and castle, the other for the splendour of huge

86

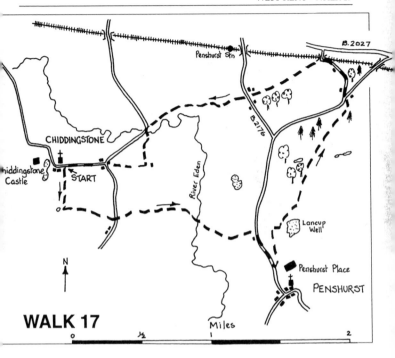

Penshurst Place and the novelty of its Tudor Leicester Square. Around them folds a peaceful, smiling countryside speckled with oasts or shaded with woodlands.

* * *

Leave the church on the left and walk along Chiddingstone (1) village street for about 50 yards. Ignore a signpost on the right directing a footpath to the Chiding Stone; a few paces beyond is a driveway and immediately after that a second footpath parallel with the drive. Walk along this path, soon to enter a large open field with views over an expanding countryside. (Chiddingstone Castle and church are seen off to the right.) The footpath leads through the field, sloping down towards some trees encircling a pond. A few paces down the left-hand side of these turn sharp left on another footpath, and at the opposite boundary cross a stile by a large oak

87

tree. The continuing path makes for the far right-hand field corner, and comes onto a country road by way of a stile set beside a gate. Turn right, and in a few yards go left over another stile into a field with a stream below to the left (Grid ref: 507446).

Walk along the left headland, then enter the next field through a gap. Continue to follow the left-hand boundary, eventually reaching a stile by a field gate. A few paces after crossing this bear left, cross a stream then veer half-right towards an arched footbridge over the River Eden. Across this turn right, pass round the end of a small woodland shaw (Clappers Shaw) and go left up a slope beside a new plantation. At the head of the slope pass a pair of dutch barns and continue ahead, now following the right-hand field boundary. In the corner of the field descend some steps onto the B2176 and walk down it (caution advised) towards Penshurst.

In about ⅓ mile pass a lodge guarding a private drive on the left (Grid ref: 525441). About 50 yards beyond this cross a stile into the grounds of Penshurst Place (2) and bear half-left across a short parkland corner. Go through a squeeze stile and over the drive to a second section of parkland. Keeping left of a cricket pitch, come to a stile about 100 yards left of the fence that surrounds a lake (Lancup Well). Entering a new section of parkland bear right to follow the boundary fence until another squeeze stile gives access to yet another enclosed area of parkland. Nearby is the ancient, half-dead Bear Oak surrounded by fencing where, it is said, the last bear in England was killed.

Continue ahead for a short distance to an avenue of trees, then bear left and walk up a slope between them. Cross a stile by a magnificent specimen of an oak, whose numerous large branches are held aloft as if to support the sky. Reaching the top of the slope veer right a few paces on a grass track, then go left over a stile to walk ahead along the left-hand edge of a plantation towards a large wood consisting mostly of conifers. A clear track leads between the dark conifer woods and a large area of coppice. At the far side come to a crossing track and bear left, sloping down to a country road. Turn left, then almost immediately head to the right on a narrow lane signposted to Chiddingstone (Grid ref: 534459).

Wander along the lane until it makes a sharp right-hand bend to cross the railway. Leave it here and walk ahead on the farm drive of

Between Chiddingstone and Penshurst the River Eden is crossed by this footbridge

Little Moorden. A few yards along this cross a stile on the right, next to a field gate, and walk along the left-hand edge of a large field. At the far side go directly ahead to walk along the edge of a hop garden, then follow a track into a farmyard. Bear left and walk up to the B2176 at Moorden Farm. Turn right, then cross a stile on the left and walk directly ahead. At the end of this first field go down a slope, bear right through a gap, then left to cross a minor stream by a field gate, over a stile and walk ahead. Find a stile in the far hedgerow about 30 yards to the right of a pillbox. Cross to another gap in the far boundary, enter the next low-lying field and walk over to the far left-hand corner where a footbridge crosses a stream into a last field with the River Eden winding to the left. Cross to Vexour Bridge where yet another stile leads onto a country road (Grid ref: 512455).

Turn left, cross the bridge and walk up a private drive. The drive curves left and immediately after passing a clump of trees hiding a hollow, break away to the right onto a footpath which climbs some steps and enters a field. Walk along the left headland. Reaching the brow of the hill bear sharp right and walk across the centre of the field towards a few trees, through which may be seen some oasts and a farm. (Views to the right over the Eden Valley to the Greensand Ridge.) On the far side of the field come onto a lane by a pond. Turn right, then bear left in front of a converted oast house occupying a tiny triangle of roads. Walk along the lane a short distance into Chiddingstone.

Items of interest:

1: Chiddingstone. The single street of Tudor houses overlooked by the church of St Mary, is owned by the National Trust. Visitors flock there at all times of the year, and the half-timbered buildings that overhang the street have been carefully filmed as an authentic background to historic dramas. The Castle Inn has been an inn since 1730, and looks it too. Next to it the ornate gates of Chiddingstone Castle provide private access to the solemn stone-encased mansion formerly known as High Street House. Originally a Tudor manor, it was almost completely demolished in 1679 by Henry Streatfeild, who then set about building a replacement in red brick. A century after this the whole thing was given a stone and battlemented façade with little fanciful turrets and towers, and the name was changed to Chiddingstone Castle. The church is surprisingly spacious to serve so small a parish, while the Chiding Stone, reached by a footpath from the village street, is said to have gained its name from the practice of visiting preachers to stand upon it and chide locals for their sinful ways.

2: Penshurst Place. Vast mellow walls stare out across the parkland. The west side is "defended" by a ha-ha, the south partly hidden behind a wall that surrounds a garden, of which Ben Jonson wrote: "Then hath thy orchard fruit, thy garden flowers,/Fresh as the ayre, and new as the houres." At the time of the Domesday Book there was a house here, but it was Sir John de Pulteney who in 1340 set the foundations for the present Penshurst Place. Its most impressive feature is the Great Hall, 60ft high with a chestnut-beamed roof. Elizabeth I was a visitor, for Sir Philip Sidney (1554-1586), poet and statesman who was born here, was a favourite of the virgin queen. The house contains portraits of Sir Philip (and many others), and mementoes of his life, and is open to the public.

WALK 18: COWDEN - HORSESHOE GREEN - BASSETTS - COWDEN

Distance:	6¹/2 miles
Maps:	OS Pathfinder TQ 44/54 Tonbridge & Edenbridge 1:25,000
	OS Landranger 188 Maidstone & The Weald of Kent 1:50,000
Start:	The Crown, Cowden High Street (Grid ref: 466405)
Access:	By signposted road off B2026 about 3 miles south of Edenbridge. Cowden is served by two bus routes: Tunbridge Wells-East Grinstead, and Edenbridge-Tunbridge Wells. Nearest station: Cowden, 1¹/2 miles.
Parking:	With discretion in the village.
Refreshments:	None on route.

Snug against the Kent-Sussex border Cowden is a small but attractive village of white weatherboarded or tile-hung cottages. It has some fine timber-framed houses too, a church with a tall shingle spire and The Crown, an inn since 1630, although it was originally built as three cottages in 1540. Surrounding the village an immaculate countryside folds in all directions, with a rich assortment of footpaths inviting exploration. Kent Water, the modest stream that forms the county boundary, flows through meadows below. Just outside Cowden there's a one-time furnace pond, and several other indications are there to serve as reminders that this was once at the heart of the Wealden iron industry.

Cowden is partially protected by a ridge. From it a beautiful panorama scans beyond the Eden Valley to the north to the Greensand Ridge and, in places, even to the North Downs beyond that. To the south another ridge rises blue on the horizon; this is Ashdown Forest, one-time royal hunting ground, in East Sussex. This walk gives opportunities to enjoy vistas to both north and south, and it is the uncluttered, undulating and unspoilt countryside that will remain firmly fixed in memory when the route has been accomplished.

* * *

With the parish church (1) on the right walk along the road for a few yards, then go left through a swing gate into a field. Take the path

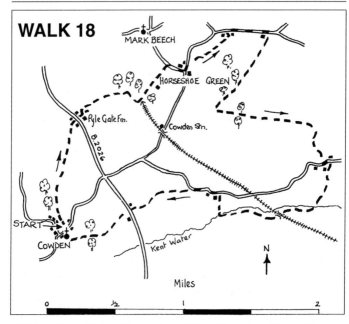

WALK 18

MARK BEECH

HORSESHOE GREEN

Pyle Gate Fm.

B 2026

Cowden Stn.

START

COWDEN

Kent Water

N

Miles

0   ½   1   2

which strikes off ahead towards a white cottage (another path veers left along the back of a row of houses). Cross the drive in front of the cottage and continue ahead alongside trees. The path leads along the edge of Jones's Wood and then forks. Bear right on the right-hand boundary of a field and descend to a stream. Cross on a sturdy footbridge and enter a large meadow. On the skyline can be seen a barn roof. The way angles across the meadow towards it, passing to the left of a tree-circled hollow. At the far side cross a stile and veer round to the right to reach another stile among a group of barns, beyond which is the B2026 road (Grid ref: 467417).

Cross straight over (with care) to Pyle Gate Farm. Through a gateway follow the drive round to the left, then bear right by farm buildings to pass a small pond. Walk down a farm track towards woodland. Eventually reach a crossing track with a cottage seen off to the left. Turn right, and when the track forks soon after (still on the edge of woods, with a stream below), bear left to walk uphill, passing a railway bridge where the line emerges from Markbeech Tunnel (2) near Cowden Station. The track narrows to a footpath among trees, then emerges below a red brick and tile-hung house named Edells. Continue uphill, passing well to the left of the house, over a squeeze stile in a stand of trees, then up the left-hand side of a sloping meadow to reach a country lane with beautiful views into Sussex (Grid ref: 476424).

Turn right and walk along the lane to a junction of roads at Horseshoe Green. Bear left and shortly after cross a stile into a field on the right. Go half-left towards the left-hand end of a line of trees and pass through a gap into the next field. Buckhurst Farm can be seen a couple of fields ahead. Walk towards it, passing close to a group of trees hiding a pond. Just beyond this a stile leads into a third field, on the far side of which the way leads through a paddock and between a converted barn (Malletts Barn) and the wall of Buckhurst Farm. Come to a drive, turn left and in a few paces join a country road and head to the right (Grid ref: 484427).

Walk along the road for about 400 yards. Immediately past Walnut Tree Cross Farm turn right along a track. When it ends bear half-right and wander down a slope to a stile among trees bordering a stream. The path traces the edge of Bilton's Gill (a woodland), then cuts off to the right to go through it. In the wood cross a footbridge over the stream, rise on the other side and emerge in a sheltered meadowland "bay". Walk ahead along the left-hand side and up the slope beyond. Near the head of the slope there is a marker post. At this turn sharp left (an elbow turn) to a hedgerow spur forming a boundary to another meadowland "bay". Go down the left-hand side of the hedgerow and into the lower edge of a wood honeycombed with rabbits' burrows and badger setts. In spring a magnificent carpet of bluebells swamps the woodland floor.

Leave the wood by a stile and continue ahead through a long meadow with more woods below to the left. Soon pass an outcrop of sandstone rocks. At the far end of the field go through a gap into another, and follow its left-hand boundary to a stile in the far corner. Over this a path winds among trees (initially very boggy), over a stream chuckling from a spring and out to a field with a glorious timber-framed house (Bassetts) seen ahead. Come onto a lane left of the house and bear left. A few paces later go to the right on a drive leading to Prinkham, another delightful timber-framed house. Just before reaching this a path cuts alongside the left-hand hedge. Pass a low barn and over a stile beyond; then veer right round the edge of a field and cross another stile into the adjacent field on the right.

Walk through the field parallel with a brook, and come to a sturdy wooden bridge over Kent Water, the stream that forms the county boundary. Cross into East Sussex and bear right (Grid ref: 495408).

Over a stile enter a large meadow and follow the stream. Shortly after crossing a ditch veer left and find a bridge through which to pass beneath a railway line, then turn right and continue alongside Kent Water through a succession of fields linked by stiles. On reaching a junction of trails bear right over a metal bridge to return to Kent. Now walk ahead along the left-hand edge of a field and come to a narrow road just to the right of Moat Farm. Bear left. Wandering along this road pass a few houses, but when it curves to the right leave the road and take a footpath on the left. This traces the left-hand edge of a large field and on the far side crosses a footbridge on the left. Go up the left headland of the next field, passing a pond enclosed by trees, and through a gap into another field. Continue ahead, now aiming towards the left-hand side of a house, to reach the B2026 road. Cross with care to a footpath on the opposite side (Grid ref: 474404).

Entering yet another large field cross half-left to find a stile leading down among trees to a stream. Cross this and leaving the trees go over the next field, through a small woodland and over more fields with Cowden's church beckoning ahead. The footpath leads directly into the churchyard.

Items of interest:

1: Cowden Parish Church. From tower to tip the 127ft spire is shingled, rising above the trees and detected from afar. The church is dedicated to St Mary Magdalene and dates from the fourteenth century, but with the north aisle added in the nineteenth. There are some lovely timbers supporting the tower, and a fine kingpost roof. In the churchyard lie local ironmasters whose industry bequeathed some handsome houses to the neighbourhood.

2: Markbeech Tunnel. The branch line from Edenbridge Town to Uckfield which passes through the tunnel was built in the 1880s for the London, Brighton and South Coast Railway.

WALK 19: GROOMBRIDGE - SPELDHURST - GROOMBRIDGE

Distance:	8¹/₂ miles (A route) 6¹/₂ miles (B route)
Maps:	OS Pathfinder TQ 44/54 Tonbridge & Edenbridge and TQ 43/53 Royal Tunbridge Wells 1:25,000
	OS Landranger 188 Maidstone & The Weald of Kent 1:50,000
Start:	The Crown Inn, Groombridge (Grid ref: 531377)
Access:	4 miles west of Tunbridge Wells, Groombridge is reached by A264 and B2110. The Crown stands beside B2110.
Parking:	Public car park south of River Grom (Grid ref: 532374).
Refreshments:	Pubs in Groombridge, Speldhurst and (A route only) Fordcombe.

Groombridge is unequally divided by the little River Grom, an early tributary of the Medway and an effective boundary between Kent and East Sussex. South of the Grom Sussex claims by far the larger part of the village, but the older and more attractive portion is grouped around a sloping triangular green in Kent. Weatherboarded or tile-hung cottages, and The Crown Inn at one end, create a charming scene. Nearby stands Groombridge Place with its open parkland, its moat and a lake to reflect a bank of rhododendrons. While this northern part of the village is unquestionably attractive, the surrounding countryside, rucked with High Wealden ridges, is likewise full of charm with long views or intimate corners, of quaint cottages, ponds bright with yellow flag in early summer, peaceful streams, bluebell woods and folding hills and vales.

Two walks are offered. As far as Bullingstone, south-west of Speldhurst, the routes are the same. But on the edge of Avery's Wood the ways divide. The "A" route continues in a south-westerly direction along part of the Wealdway, and is the longer option; the "B" route strikes off southward

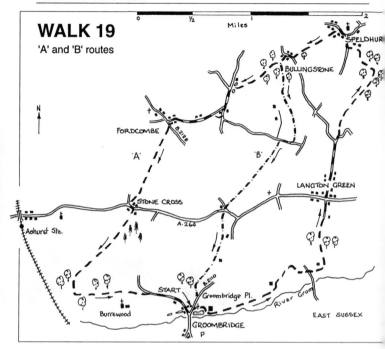

WALK 19

'A' and 'B' routes

N

SPELDHUR

BULLINGSTONE

FORDCOMBE

'A'   'B'

LANGTON GREEN

STONE CROSS

A.264

Aohurst Stn.

START

Groombridge Pl.

River Grom

Burrswood

EAST SUSSEX

GROOMBRIDGE
P

*and offers a more direct return to Groombridge. Route "A" provides
striking views south of Stone Cross, but involves more road walking, while
route "B" teases over meadows with hinted views to a blue distance. Both
are worth tackling.*

*   *   *

From The Crown cross the B2110, go through a gate and along a
footpath beside a churchyard into parkland. The way is clearly
defined and leads across a drive, along the eastern edge of a lake,
round the southern side of the moat surrounding Groombridge
Place (1), then divides. Ignore that which breaks off to the right and
continue ahead, through a gate and across a large field with the
River Grom marking its right-hand boundary. Enter and cross a
second field to a footbridge over a ditch. Beyond this walk ahead
along the right-hand side of a row of pollarded willows. The way

Scotney Castle, one of the great romantic sites of Kent *(Walk 26)*

The nineteenth-century smock mill towers over Cranbrook's weatherboarded shops and cottages *(Walk 27)*
A novel clapper stile at Tenterden *(Walk 32)*

then veers left towards the farm buildings of Pokehill. Across the farm drive the path bears left between fences, then right guided by hedgerows. Pass a sewage works on the right and continue between fences to reach a narrow lane. Cross over and continue on a track which forks near the entrance to Adams Well, a cottage on the left. Leave the track and continue ahead, sloping down to a bridge over a stream, then bear left on a sunken track that rises among trees. Eventually come to a lane (Barrow Lane) and walk along it to the A264 at Langton Green (Grid ref: 550392).

Cross with care and walk along Farnham Lane, at first lined with houses, then easing into countryside with Speldhurst church glimpsed some way ahead. A little over 1/2 mile from the main road a minor lane goes left towards Speldhurst. Ignore this and continue for about 250 yards. As the lane curves to the right, leave it and cross a stile next to a field gate and walk ahead down a sloping meadow to a stream. (Farm buildings to the right.) Over the stream continue slightly left to pass round the foot of a hill, then over another stile into mixed woodland, at first among bushes of broom. At a crossing path keep ahead, walking parallel with the stream. The footpath is joined by another from the right. It then veers left, rises uphill and forks. Take the left-hand option, soon sloping down to the stream which is crossed on a footbridge. Rise up on the western side and leave the woods to walk across an open meadow between fences. This leads to a drive, which in turn goes to a road. Turn right and walk towards the Parish Church in Speldhurst (2).

At a T junction of roads in front of the church turn left (Grid ref: 554414). The road curves to the right, and shortly after go left through a swing gate by a footpath sign (to Bullingstone Lane). This path leads alongside a wooden fence, then hedges, and comes to a large open field with big views westward. Now on the route of the Wealdway (3) walk across the centre of the field to a long woodland shaw which leads directly to Bullingstone Lane (Grid ref: 545412).

Bear right along the lane, passing an old farmhouse, then turn left by a lovely little thatched cottage (Old Bullingstone), where a tight footpath enclosed by hedges leads to Avery's Wood. At the entrance to the wood the path forks.

Route A (the longer option) continues on the Wealdway and takes the right-hand path. Descend to a stream, cross a footbridge and wind on through the woods. When the way forks bear right to climb uphill, eventually emerging into a meadow which is crossed well to the left of a farmhouse. Cross another meadow to the far left corner, enter a small wood between a couple of ponds and come onto a lane. Bear left. Pass Silcocks Farm at a road junction and continue ahead for another 50 yards. Turn right on a footpath near some outbuildings, then across a small meadow to the top corner where a stile leads onto a lane. Bear left along it for about a third of a mile to reach Fordcombe and the B2188 (Grid ref: 527403).

Cross the road and walk round the left-hand edge of a cricket pitch to its far corner where the continuing footpath goes along the left headland of several large fields on the way to Stone Cross. (Fine broad views of an undulating countryside, a patchwork of fields, meadows and woods; to the north the Greensand Ridge marks a far horizon, while the heights of Ashdown Forest do the same to the south-west.)

Come to a group of cottages and converted oast houses at Stone Cross. Bear left on the A264 (caution advised) for about 60 yards. As the road bends left, take a footpath on the right which leads alongside a house, then past stables before entering a long, narrow meadow with larchwoods on the left. Walk ahead; views become broad and very lovely. Come to a stile by a field gate, enter the next meadow and continue ahead, keeping near the head of the slope. On the far boundary cross the left-hand of two stiles and go down the right-hand edge of a meadow. Half-way down cross another stile into the adjacent field on the right and continue downhill. Go through a narrow woodland, leave the route of the Wealdway and turn left towards the far corner of a field and a gap between two patches of woodland. Cross a stile and go over the centre of a field towards yet another woodland. Walk uphill through it, and emerging bear half-right to the far corner of another field. Wind among scrubland and reach a private drive leading to Burrswood (4). Cross the drive and a final field to gain a narrow lane. Bear right and walk down to Groombridge.

Route B takes the left-hand path down into Avery's Wood. Cross a plank footbridge over a stream and wander up the slope. Marker posts guide the route (recently diverted), through the woods. Come to a distinctive Y junction and take the right branch, which soon widens and leaves the woods through a field gate. Continue on the left-hand side of a meadow to the far side where a stile has been created out of a tree trunk. Cross the drive leading to Danemore Park and go ahead along the left-hand side of a second meadow. In the far corner cross a stile on the left and bear right alongside the field boundary to a country road (Grid ref: 545400).

Turn right for almost 200 yards, and just before reaching the entrance drive to Danemore Farm, head to the left over a stile and along the left-hand side of a field. At the far corner bear right for a few paces, then go through a squeeze stile and half-right across a meadow towards a brick barn. Cross the drive to Shirley Hall (the white building seen to the right) and continue ahead. Pass to the left of the brick barn, go over two stiles and along the right-hand edge of a meadow with a sports ground seen to the left. Cross a second drive (to Ashurst Place), continue ahead slightly to the right to a squeeze stile, and over this maintain direction through a series of meadows linked by stiles, following waymarks of the High Weald Walk.

Come to the junction of A264 and B2188 by Langton Lodge (Grid ref: 535390), whose chimneys could just be seen among trees whilst crossing the final stretch of meadow. Cross both roads and, leaving the High Weald Walk, go over a stile and walk ahead through a large field to its far corner by some houses. Come to a junction of trails and once more join the High Weald Walk. Continue ahead slightly right on a track, which soon forks. Take the left branch. It leads to Top Hill Farm and on the way there are glimpsed views to the rise of Ashdown Forest.

At the right-hand end of farm buildings join a farm road. This leads to a crossing concrete road. Bear right and in a few paces leave it to go down the left-hand side of a field, enter a woodland at the bottom corner and follow the path winding downhill (rich with bluebells in spring). Out of the woods continue down the slope to the B2110, then turn right and walk into Groombridge.

Items of interest:

1: Groombridge Place. This Charles II manor house with its own moat occupies the site of a castle built by a Saxon, Gromen, from whom Groombridge takes its name. A Norman castle replaced

Gromen's, but the present house dates from the early seventeenth century.

2: Speldhurst. The village was mentioned in a document dated AD768, a trim place on a Wealden ridge on the fringe of the former iron-making region. The church is a Victorian replacement of a Norman place of worship that burned down in 1791 after being struck by lightning. The George and Dragon nearby, half-timbered and handsome, is said to originate from the thirteenth century.

3: The Wealdway. An 82-mile long-distance route that begins in Gravesend on the Thames and ends at Beachy Head on the Sussex Coast. Guidebook: *The Wealdway & the Vanguard Way* by Kev Reynolds (Cicerone Press 1987)

4: Burrswood. To the west of Groombridge, on the north bank of the Grom, Burrswood is a Christian centre for medical and spiritual care.

WALK 2O: SHIPBOURNE - UNDERRIVER - IGHTHAM MOTE - SHIPBOURNE

Distance:	6 miles
Maps:	OS Pathfinder TQ 45/55 Sevenoaks & Westerham 1:25,000
	OS Landranger 188 Maidstone & The Weald of Kent 1:50,000
Start:	Shipbourne church (Grid ref: 592523)
Access:	By A227 about 3^{1}/2 miles north of Tonbridge.
Parking:	By the church, or in a lay-by on Upper Green Road opposite.
Refreshments:	Pubs in Shipbourne and Underriver (100yds off route)

The vast expanse and wooded splendours of the Weald are displayed during this walk. Shipbourne, where it begins, lies below the greensand hills which form a protective wall to the north, and this circular outing explores a section of its ridge. But first there are the open fields and meadows, the woods and woodland shaws of the Weald to enjoy. There are a few grand houses too, and others, perhaps less obviously grand, but no less splendidly

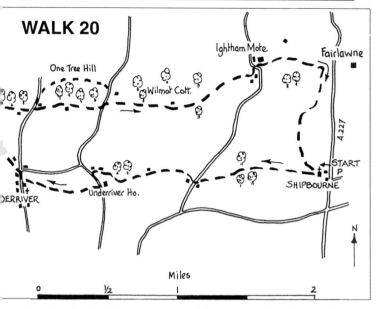

WALK 20

One Tree Hill

Wilmot Cott.

Ightham Mote

Fairlawne

A.227

START
P

SHIPBOURNE

DERRIVER

Underriver Ho.

N

Miles

0   ½   1   2

placed, perched as they are on the southern slopes of the ridge with all the world, it would seem, spread below their gardens. Yet the finest of them all is unquestionably the medieval manor house of Ightham Mote, a real architectural gem in the care of the National Trust. Our walk passes alongside its moat.

* * *

Walk through Shipbourne (1) churchyard and out by way of a swing gate in the western wall to a field where three footpaths begin. Take the central path cutting ahead across two adjoining fields to reach the right-hand end of a woodland, shown as Cold Blows on the 2½" map. Enter the wood and take the right-hand of two paths, soon rising up an easy slope to a view of the Greensand Ridge. The path forks. Bear left, still rising among larches, and at the top of the slope gain a view over the Weald. The path continues, now easing downhill, and before long comes onto a narrow country road beside Budds Oast (Grid ref: 577522). Bear left for about 30 yards, then turn right along Great Budds driveway. Pass to the right

101

of the house, then continue on a stony track which goes ahead beside a large black barn.

Beyond the garden boundary of Great Budds enter a field with the Greensand Ridge again rising off to the right, and with Wilmot Cottage (2), which we pass later, clearly seen on the slope to the north.

Entering a second field leave the track and take a footpath directly ahead to a brief woodland shaw. Go through it and across a third field towards a pair of barns. Walk along the left-hand side of these and into another field, now with woods to the right and Underriver House seen ahead. At the end of the field cross a stile, bear right and walk towards another field gate. Do not pass through it, but turn left along a footpath enclosed by two close-growing rows of cypress trees leading to a driveway. Continue ahead, passing several houses, and reach a country road (Grid ref: 565523).

Turn left, and about 100 yards later (in front of Underriver House) cross a stile on the right and walk across a field to a second stile by a field gate on the edge of a small copse. The way continues ahead aiming towards a pair of oak trees with a stile nearby. Maintaining direction (fine views, particularly to the right) come to a row of poplars. The footpath goes alongside these and reaches another road in the small village of Underriver (Grid ref: 556524). Note: if refreshments are needed at this point, The White Rock Inn is found 100 yards to the left.

Turn right for about 100 yards, then bear left along a drive by Valley Farm, coloured in spring by ornamental cherry trees. When it curves right at Black Charles (a house), leave the drive and continue on a bridleway. This narrows on the uphill approach to some oast houses. A few paces before meeting a drive, bear right to walk along the right-hand side of the oasts, then go up a delightful sunken track providing snatched views through the trees to the Weald and along the sweeping Greensand Ridge.

Near the head of the slope come to a crossing path (Greensand Way) and bear right. With woodland on the left and magnificent views to the right the walk enters its second phase; the hillside route. Soon views are restricted for a short spell, then the path comes to a drive and onto a very narrow road (Grid ref: 557529). Two options are available; "A" follows the Greensand Way over One Tree Hill,

"B" continues on a track a little lower. Both enjoy good, but different, views and converge again at the next narrow road crossing below Rooks Hill House.

Route A turns left up the road for a short distance, then bears right (Greensand Way marker) to climb among trees and bushes onto the National Trust owned One Tree Hill. On the highest point there is a seat with beautiful and far-reaching views. Continue ahead, soon sloping downhill among trees, at times very steeply (take care in wet conditions), and eventually come to a very narrow road near Rooks Hill House. Wander down the road for a few yards, then go left on the waymarked footpath, rejoining option B.

Route B leaves the Greensand Way and turns right, then almost immediately heads to the left along a track with more fine views. When it forks take the left branch rising to White Rocks Farm. Pass along the left-hand side of the house and continue on a footpath that winds an undulating course among trees, then reaches another very narrow lane. Cross over and rejoin Route A and the continuing Greensand Way.

Routes A and B having converged the path enters more National Trust land and soon enjoys fine views again. Reach Wilmot Cottage (Grid ref: 574529). (Note: an alternative footpath here heads to the right and offers a shorter return to Shipbourne via Budds Oast and Cold Blows.) Follow a track which goes ahead from Wilmot Cottage, passes between patches of bluebell woods (mixed with massed stars of wild garlic in spring) and eventually reaches Mote Farm. Bear left at the farm and come to yet another country road. Head to the right and a few paces later turn left (leaving the Greensand Way) into the drive of Ightham Mote (3).

Walk alongside the moat and continue rising uphill. Go beyond the car park entrance, now on a track between fields. It narrows beside a hedgerow and comes to a field gate with a large house called Fairlawne (4) seen ahead. Bear right along the edge of a field and come to another field gate. Maintain direction, soon sloping downhill to pass along the left headland of a field which borders a cricket pitch. The way continues without difficulty to Shipbourne church seen ahead.

Items of interest:

1: Shipbourne. This small but straggling village provides the starting point for several fine walks. At its heart stands the church of St Giles, with The Chaser Inn and some tile-hung cottages nearby. The present church, Early English in style, is a Victorian reconstruction with gargoyles projecting from the tower. At the lychgate is a coffin rest, while inside the church lies Sir Henry Vane - see Note 4 below.

2: Wilmot Cottage. It is said that this cottage, with its beautiful Wealden views, was once an ale-house when the trackway past its door was a pack-horse route.

3: Ightham Mote. Begun around 1340 this magnificent manor house with its duck-dabbling moat is now in the hands of the National Trust. (The Mote of its name refers to its having been a meeting place - or moot - and is not a mis-spelling of the waterway round it.) The house boasts a Great Hall, two chapels, a crypt, and a pair of solars, and is well worth visiting.

4: Fairlawne. This large grey mansion set above lake-sprinkled grounds to the north of Shipbourne village was once owned by Sir Henry Vane who was executed on Tower Hill for supporting the Roundheads. He now lies in a vault in the village church. Footpaths lead through parkland surrounding the house and emerge on the edge of Plaxtol.

WALK 21: PLATT - PLAXTOL SPOUTE - GOVER HILL - PLATT

Distance:	8 miles
Maps:	OS Pathfinder TQ 65/75 Maidstone 1:25,000
	OS Landranger 188 Maidstone & The Weald of Kent 1:50,000
Start:	Church of St Mary the Virgin, Platt (Grid ref: 623570)
Access:	By minor road south of A25 just east of Borough Green.
Parking:	With discretion in the village.
Refreshments:	Pubs in Platt, Basted and Dunks Green (400yds off route).

South of the A25 at Borough Green the greensand hills are speckled with orchards, hop gardens and fields of soft fruit; a benevolent patch of country criss-crossed with narrow winding lanes and footpaths, and with the clear stream of the River Bourne gliding peacefully among the meadows, no longer required to power mills near Dunks Green, as it did in the past. Three long distance walks pass through: the Wealdway, London Countryway and the Greensand Way. Small villages and hamlets provide a smattering of community life, while farms and farm cottages look directly to the land. Overlooking it all from rising ground to the east Mereworth Woods provide a vast dark crown. This route picks out some of the best this countryside has to offer, enjoying meadows, orchards and woodland, as well as following the Bourne stream for a short stretch. A little longer than most walks in this book, it will reward several hours of exploration. Take a packed lunch and amble leisurely along giving time here and there to enjoy the views.

*   *   *

The walk begins south of the village church in Platt (1) and goes down Long Mill Lane for about 300 yards before heading to the right on a bridleway between two handsome half-timbered houses, and into a field. Follow a hedgerow with views to the North Downs; after edging two fields come to a farm road and continue ahead as far as a country lane (Grid ref: 616564).

Cross over, go through a narrow woodland shaw and turn left on a crossing path (not shown on the OS map). Shortly before reaching a cottage the path swings to the right and soon traces the right-hand edge of Long Bottom Wood. Before long enter the wood, descend a slope, wander through a meadow between woods, and eventually arrive in Basted beside an office block (Grid ref: 606558). Turn left along a narrow road. Over the River Bourne (2) go uphill to The Plough. Beside the pub sign cross a stile and walk along an enclosed footpath to a large open field. The continuing path goes through the field to reach Winfield Lane by the side of a small woodland.

Cross the lane and continue ahead along the right-hand edge of another field to a lane almost opposite Bourne Farm. Bear left for a few paces, then between a barn and a farmhouse head to the right through a gate into the farmyard. Passing a pond on the left a track rises between trees, then goes along the left headland of a large field.

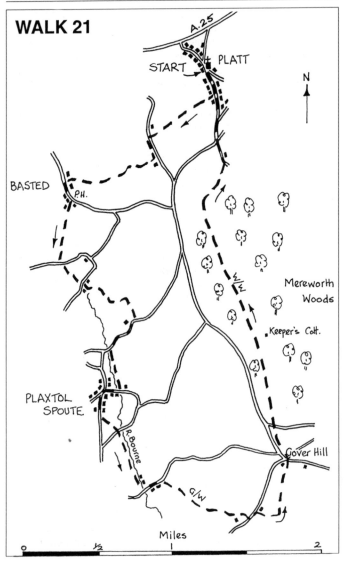

WALK 21

A.25

START PLATT

N

BASTED

P.H.

Mereworth
Woods

Keeper's Cott.

PLAXTOL
SPOUTE

R.Bourne

Gover Hill

C/W

Miles

0   ½   1   2

About 100 yards along this field break away to the right and cross to the opposite hedgerow and a stile. Enter an orchard and turn left along its boundary. At the end bear right, still along the boundary, then round the edge of an adjacent field. During research for this guide the field was divided by a wooden fence to create a paddock, and there was no stile nor gate giving access into it. In the left-hand corner of the paddock (well to the left of a converted oast house, Long Mill Farm) a stile leads onto another country road (Grid ref: 615544) just east of the path shown on the OS map.

Bear right. The lane twists past the farm entrance, goes downhill a little and beneath power lines. Just beyond these enter the field on the left and follow the Bourne stream. At the far side of the field come to a junction of paths. (That which heads to the left goes to Old Soar Manor (3).) Cross the stile directly ahead, go along the right-hand edge of the next field, then join another narrow road. Turn right into Plaxtol Spoute. At a junction of roads bear left, and left again beside a handsome fifteenth-century timber-framed building used as the showroom of Hyders Ltd, art metal workers. About 150 yards beyond the last house in Plaxtol Spoute cross a stile on the left next to a field gate and walk across this field to its far right-hand corner to rejoin the River Bourne.

Cross yet another narrow lane and continue ahead along the edge of two fields. Two thirds of the way along the second of these follow a fenced path by the side of the stream, on the other side of which is Roughway Mill (4). Come to another lane and bear left (Grid ref: 615526). (Should you be in need of refreshment The Kentish Rifleman pub is found about 400 yards to the right, in Dunks Green.)

Walk up the road to pass a row of houses, immediately after which cross a stile on the right and follow waymarks for the Greensand Way. Walk uphill diagonally through an orchard, bear right for a few paces, then enter a sloping field. Go down the left-hand edge, and near the bottom pass through the boundary on the left and continue across the lower corner of this field. Cross a ditch and bear left; then recross it to wind round field boundaries with waymarks guiding the route. Cross another stile and head up a sloping meadow with a converted oast house at the top. The way leads along the left-hand boundary of the house garden, then by way of a farm track reaches a country road (Grid ref: 626524).

Bear left and in a few paces go right up some steps beside a house. The footpath leads between a fence and a tall hedge to reach a crossing track. Leave the Greensand Way and turn left, now on the Wealdway rising between fences (lovely views behind) to a junction of narrow roads at Gover Hill (Grid ref: 631529). Almost directly ahead a path enters Mereworth Woods (5) next to a National Trust sign.

The path soon divides by some large beech trees. Take the left fork, come to a narrow metalled lane and cross directly ahead on a broad forest track going through mostly coppiced woodland. In ³/₄ mile from Gover Hill reach a major junction of tracks not far from Keepers Cottage (just seen to the right); continue straight ahead and remain on this obvious route through the woods, here known as Shipbourne Forest, ignoring alternative paths. Eventually the track narrows and comes to an opening of woods with an orchard on the left giving distant views towards Plaxtol. The path then edges between fields and woods and eases down to a narrow country road. Walk along this, then join Long Mill Lane which leads to Platt in ¹/₂ mile.

Items of interest:

1: Platt. Rarely mentioned in Kentish books, the village has a number of lovely half-timbered houses and attractive cottages. The nearby gardens of Great Comp are open to the public. Platt is a local word for orchards of Kentish cobnuts, of which there are some on either side of Long Mill Lane.

2: River Bourne. The banks of this innocent stream, a tributary of the Medway, were settled in the Bronze Age, Iron Age and by the Romans too. On the approach to Roughway, near Dunks Green, our walk passes the site of a Roman villa where a statue of Minerva was found.

3: Old Soar Manor. In the care of the National Trust, this small ragstone manor dates from 1290 but has a red-brick Georgian farmhouse attached. Old Soar consists of a first-floor solar, chapel and undercrofts. The farmhouse is built on what was the original hall, and is private.

4: Roughway Mill. This mill on the little River Bourne near Dunks Green produced high quality paper from the early nineteenth century. Among its uses were bank notes, stamps and postal orders.

5: Mereworth Woods. One of the largest woodlands left in Kent, Mereworth Woods cover an area of almost 6 square miles. During Elizabethan times wild boar were hunted there. Today the woods are in the ownership of the Forestry Commission, Ministry Defence, some private, and a small area at Gover Hill, by the National Trust.

WALK 22: TESTON BRIDGE - WATERINGBURY - KETTLE BRIDGE - TESTON

Distance:	3 miles (A route) 5½ miles (B route)
Maps:	OS Pathfinder TQ 65/75 Maidstone 1:25,000
	OS Landranger 188 Maidstone & The Weald of Kent 1:50,000
Start:	Teston Bridge Picnic Site (Grid ref: 707532)
Access:	By B2163 signposted from A26 about 4 miles west of Maidstone.
Parking:	Teston Bridge Picnic Site.
Refreshments:	Pub and restaurant/cafe in Wateringbury.

Teston Bridge is one of four splendid medieval ragstone bridges on the Medway; the others are at Yalding, East Farleigh and Aylesford. Nearby a lock, a weir and the remains of an old mill reflected in the water form an attractive group. Teston Bridge Picnic Site comes down to the river at this point. There is a car park, public toilet, picnic tables - and three meadows which prove extremely popular throughout the summer. KCC manages the 32-acre site, and from time to time special events are held there and guided walks arranged from it.

Although this is the only Medway walk contained in this book, the river bank provides plenty of opportunities for A to B linear routes along the towpath, as well as assorted circular walks. KCC has produced a slim pack of towpath guide leaflets (River Valley Walks in Kent - River Medway) and a guidebook to the River Medway Path which describes the course of the navigation from Tonbridge to Rochester. It's a fascinating river, and

WALK 22

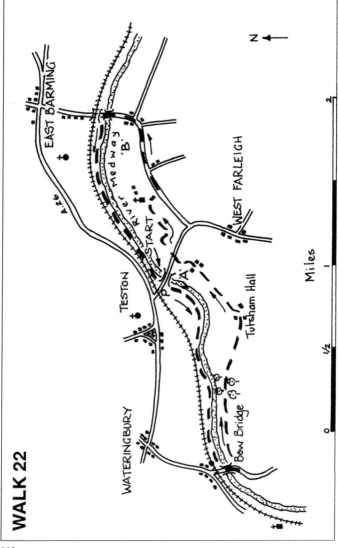

EAST BARMING

A.26

TESTON

River Medway 'B'

START

'A'

Tutsham Hall

WATERINGBURY

Bow Bridge

WEST FARLEIGH

N

Miles

0   ½   1   2

Teston Bridge, one of the four medieval ragstone bridges on the Medway

the walk described here shows several of its faces. In effect there are two walks in one on offer, both of which are circular.

* * *

Cross the picnic site to the riverside and bear right along the towpath, in effect heading upstream. The path is clear and uncomplicated, and in a little under 1¹/₂ miles reaches Bow bridge at Wateringbury (1). On the approach to Wateringbury the Medway takes on a holiday atmosphere with lots of river craft moored alongside. (The Railway Inn is a short distance to the right, while a cafe/restaurant offers refreshment on the upstream side of the bridge.)

Go over the bridge to the south side of the river, then bear left, cross a cattle grid and a stile next to a field gate and walk ahead through a low-lying meadow. Over another stile enter a second meadow and continue parallel with the left-hand fence. On the far side a footbridge over a ditch gives access to a third meadow, with Waregraves Wood seen ahead. Make towards the left-hand end of the wood and wander through it on a track.

Come out of the wood and continue ahead for a few paces, then veer slightly right to rise round a shoulder of hillside. The way continues over a stile next to a field gate, then heads towards a grey barn. Pass along the left-hand side of the barn on a track leading to a farm. Go through the farmyard and up a slope, then through a field gate on the left. (On the right will be seen Tutsham Hall. Grid ref: 706526)

Now follow a narrow metalled drive round the hillside above the Medway, soon with views down to Teston Lock (2) with the bridge beyond. Pass alongside a row of white weatherboarded cottages and continue ahead. The drive dips by a pond, then rises again to pass beside a massive handsome oak tree (on the right). Soon after come to a crossing road, the B2163 (Grid ref: 710533). The shorter circuit (**A route**) turns left here and descends to Teston Bridge.

The longer circuit (**B route**) crosses the road, goes up a few steps and over a stile, then continues ahead between fences. At the end of the fenced section turn right and walk along the headland of a rectangular field. On coming to the top of it bear left and at the next corner cross a stile and maintain direction. There are two paths; ours continues ahead and shortly after enters a cricket ground. Walk along the left-hand edge with West Farleigh Church (3) just ahead. On reaching a metalled lane near the church turn right and walk up to the Yalding-Maidstone road (Grid ref: 716534).

Turn left along the footpath that accompanies the road for $^1/_2$ mile, passing orchards that obscure views of the river, and come to St Helen's Lane which drops away to the left between houses. Walk down this lane, which steepens on the approach to Kettle Bridge (also known as Barming, or St Helen's Bridge), the only timber road bridge over the Medway. Cross the river and bear left over a stile by a field gate, then follow the towpath through pleasant meadows back to Teston Bridge.

Items of interest:

1: Wateringbury. The Parish Clerk, Edward Greensted, left a vivid account of a terrible storm that raged over the village on 19 August 1763. In its wake "...how shocking was the prospect! Our houses flowing with water, scarcely a pane of glass to be seen, the roofs and

Kettle Bridge is the only timber bridge on the Medway

From the narrow drive near Tutsham Hall a fine view overlooks Teston Lock

walls of our houses shatter'd, the waters roaring in torrents down the streets, the surface of the earth covered with the prodigious hailstones and water, the corn, fruit and hops destroy'd." These hailstones were indeed "prodigious" for some measured 10 inches in diameter and many still lay in heaps more than a month later.

2: Teston Lock. The original lock was built in 1740 by the Medway Navigation Company and is one of ten positioned along the river between Tonbridge and Allington. It was rebuilt in 1911, and the lock gates (weighing over 3 tons each) were renewed in 1988. The weir next to it was once used as an eel trap, while the ruins of Tutsham Mill on the right bank of the river are all that remain of a one-time oil mill (linseed oil being produced here) destroyed by fire in 1885. The central arch of medieval Teston Bridge was rebuilt in 1749 in order to improve navigation for barges. Further rebuilding work on three other arches took place in 1830.

3: West Farleigh Church. A large part of All Saints, West Farleigh, dates from around 1100, although the Domesday Book records a church here before that. Next to it, in an idyllic setting, stands the lovely half-timbered Court Lodge Farm.

The Body of Kent

THE WEALD AND ITS BORDERS

South and east of the Medway the Low Weald spreads broad and flat, a rich chequerboard of farmland from which orchards and hop gardens burst with life in ordered rows. Farm ponds and hammer ponds lie in hollows surrounded by trees. Minor streams drift through beds of clay, draining to the Medway or the Teise or the Beult. Oast houses dot the landscape like sparkling white punctuation marks and heavy-beamed farms lean with the weight of centuries.

But the Weald is not all flat. This body of Kent has its muscular hills too, and is rucked and rumpled with ridges that stretch like limbs above hollow coombes and minor vales. On those hills squat villages like Brenchley and Goudhurst. In their hollows nestle such places as Lamberhurst and Little Chart, on land that once was dense with forest or swamp.

Anderida, this great forest that for centuries formed such an obstacle to communication, was gradually cleared as its timber was required for house building, ship building, for fuel and for the charcoal that fired the Wealden iron industry's furnaces. Some of the earliest clearings (dens) were made by settlers who needed space for agriculture. In the untamed acres there were "herds of deer and droves of hogs only". Here the Saxons grubbed out a hardy existence and their pigs grew fat among the tree roots.

And yet the Weald retains many gracious woodlands, and is today one of the most heavily wooded parts of all southern England. Not far from Cranbrook is Hempstead Forest, with more than 1,000 acres of mixed woodland. To the south of Goudhurst Bedgebury Forest spreads its 2,300-acre carpet of greenery, while the adjoining Pinetum contains Europe's largest collection of conifers with more than 200 species standing proud above and through a series of shallow valleys that remind us of elegant parklands.

The Weald has its fair share of parkland too. One of the finest is that which flanks the Scotney estate near Lamberhurst. In the midst of it, in a glorious hollow surrounded by a collection of exotic trees and shrubs, stands Scotney Castle, its ruins casting romantic reflections in the moat. There's parkland at Leeds (with its fabulous castle resting on two little islands in its lake); parkland near Pembury and Benenden, near Lenham and on the edge of Tenterden.

Tenterden vies with Cranbrook for title of Capital of the Weald. Perched on the last bit of Wealden level before the land slopes to Romney Marsh, Tenterden is a town of broad streets, handsome houses and shop fronts, a fine church and a steam railway that chunters through a lovely patch of countryside on its way to Sussex. The Marsh lies below, criss-crossed with drainage ditches and meandering reed-lined channels.

It was the cloth trade that brought prosperity to Tenterden and to Cranbrook, and both these small towns reflect that prosperity in their buildings today. Cranbrook's church is spacious and dates from the fifteenth century, when the manufacture of cloth had become established there. The town was well-situated for the trade, since a number of streams nearby could be harnessed to power the fulling mills needed as part of that industry. One of the walks in this section gives an opportunity to explore aspects of that not-quite-forgotten past.

Cranbrook's windmill is one of its best-known features, but the county as a whole is rich in windmills, as well as watermills. A modern-day windmill (a slender wind-powered generator) is seen on another of our walks, this one starting from Doddington. Doddington is not in the Weald, of course, but tucked in a gorgeous valley scooped from the North Downs to the east of Maidstone. The North Downs rim the Weald as they curve towards Canterbury, and as if to mimic their progress, the greensand hills do likewise.

While the greensand hills formed an important part of the previous section of walks, the continuing ridge down towards Ashford is included here. Along the ridge (traced for much of its length by the Greensand Way) some of the finest panoramas in all Kent are enjoyed, and routes are teased along it via Linton, Ulcombe, Boughton Malherbe, Egerton and Pluckley. There's not a dull mile along that ridge.

Throughout the county village churches create focal points for the community. Not surprisingly, since Christianity first came to

The flint-walled Norman church of St Mary at Eastling, snug among the downs.
(Walk 31)

Britain via Kentish shores, there are some very old churches indeed. Many of our walks pass close to them; some wander through their churchyards, others are spied from afar - a spire or a tower glimpsed across the green acres. A number of remote churches unfortunately need to be locked against vandalism, but there's hardly one that is open that will not repay a brief visit. That at Tudeley (Walk 23) will surprise with its extravagant stained glass. Chichester Cathedral boasts a window by the Russian artist, Marc Chagall. The tiny, easy-to-miss church at Tudeley has no less than a dozen!

An English country church is very much part of the quintessential English landscape. The quintessential landscape of Kent demands a white-tipped oast, a fluff of apple blossom, grazing sheep - and a footpath winding into the distance. The Weald has more than its fair share of each of these essentials.

* * *

THE BODY OF KENT COUNTRY PARKS AND OPEN SPACES IN THE WEALD

1:   Bewl Water: This, the largest inland water between London and the south coast, covers 770 acres (most of it in East Sussex). Recreation and picnic areas, nature reserve (entry by permit only), water sports and footpaths. Access from A21 ³/₄ mile south of Lamberhurst.

2:   Bedgebury Pinetum and Forest: The Pinetum contains Europe's finest collection of conifers in a charming series of small valleys. Visitor Centre open weekends and holidays, April-October. Bedgebury Forest, adjacent to the Pinetum, covers 2,300 acres. Access via B2079, 3 miles south of Goudhurst.

3:   Hempstead Forest, Cranbrook: More than 1,000 acres of mixed woodland to the east of Cranbrook. Car park and picnic area, reached by minor road north of Benenden.

4:   Park Wood, Kenardington: Especially fine in bluebell time, 80 acres of woodland with footpaths and splendid views from the edges. About 4¹/₂ miles east of Tenterden. On the Woodchurch-Appledore road.

5:   Faggs Wood, Orlestone: 350 acres of mixed woodland. 4¹/₂ miles south of Ashford, west of A2070.

6:   Hothfield Common Picnic Site: 140 acres of heathland and woods. Nature trail, picnic site. About 3 miles north-west of Ashford, reached from the A20.

WALK 23: TUDELEY - CAPEL - KENT COLLEGE - TUDELEY

Distance:	5 miles
Maps:	OS Pathfinder TQ 64/74 Paddock Wood & Staplehurst 1:25,000
	OS Landranger 188 Maidstone & The Weald of Kent 1:50,000
Start:	Tudeley church (Grid ref: 622454)
Access:	On the B2017 about 2½ miles east of Tonbridge.
Parking:	Beside the church.
Refreshments:	Pubs at Tudeley and near Five Oak Green.

Overlooking the Medway valley the insignificant-looking church of All Saints at Tudeley reveals itself to be anything but 'obscure and unfrequented' (as described by Hasted, the Kent historian, in 1798), for each of its windows contains the work of Marc Chagall, the internationally-famous artist and master in the craft of stained glass, who died in 1985. Such is Chagall's reputation that Tudeley now draws visitors from far and wide, for here, surprisingly, in a church that virtually stands in a farmyard with low-lying agricultural land spreading away from it, is Britain's finest collection of Chagall's work.

Thus is the scene set for this walk; a walk that makes a circuit of agricultural countryside, some of it plush with orchards or hop gardens, some of it grazed by sheep, some of it thick woodland, that links farms and two other churches that once served small communities but now stand silent witness to the past.

* * *

Begin by walking through Tudeley churchyard (1) heading east, then straight ahead across several fields as far as Bank Farm. The path leads along the right-hand side of some barns and onto a narrow lane in front of the farm. Turn left along the lane, then leave it for a track on the right opposite some oast houses. Pass an orchard, and beyond this continue in the same direction across an open field to a gap in the hedge opposite. Go through the gap and bear right, and a few paces later bear left round the edge of a small woodland. Continue ahead across a section of field, passing beneath power

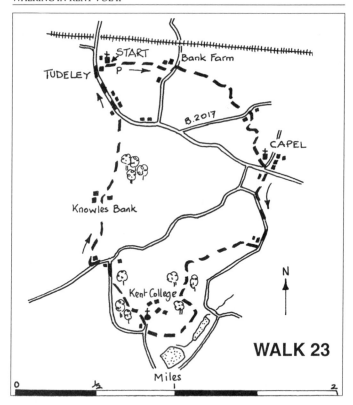

TUDELEY

START
P →

Bank Farm

B.2017

CAPEL

Knowles Bank

Kent College

N

WALK 23

0   ½   Miles   1   2

cables, and reach a group of trees. Go round these and bear right to walk alongside a hop garden as far as Five Oak Green Road (B2017) opposite The George and Dragon pub (Grid ref: 635449).

Bear left in front of the pub, and after a few paces take a footpath on the right which goes through a woodland shaw and comes to a stile at the corner of a field. Over the stile follow the left-hand boundary, then bear right in the far corner, still with the boundary on the left with a large hop garden beyond. At the first opportunity slant half-left across to Capel Church (2). The route passes through the churchyard a little to the right of the building (worth a visit, if open) and exits at a junction of roads. Bear right and cross the road to a farm track passing to the left of a large black barn. Soon after this note the old hoppers' huts to the left of the track, formerly used to accommodate hop-pickers from London during the hop harvest, before picking was done mechanically.

The track rises a little and passes a small fence-enclosed copse, planted in memory of a local farmer by the employees of Church Farm, Capel, the fence donated by former London hop-pickers. Come to a narrow country lane and turn left along it, passing orchards. On reaching a pair of houses on the right of the lane, turn right immediately beyond them on a short drive, and through a small orchard to a stile by a field gate. Cross the stile and bear left along the headland of a field. In the corner come to another stile and a junction of paths. Continue directly ahead through a succession of orchards. When these end turn right in a field by a pond, cross a stile among trees, and bear left to follow the left-hand edge of a large field, keeping alert for a stile which leads into a woodland shaw.

Enter the shaw which edges a stream. A wood soon spreads off to the left, and eventually the path crosses the stream (masses of wild garlic in spring) by a footbridge, and goes up the opposite bank. The way continues winding through the woods and comes to a field gate. Do not go through it, but bear left along a broad path following a fence on the right. Come to a stile giving access to a meadow on the right. Walk ahead over this open meadow towards a field gate with a stile next to it, and with the complex of buildings of Kent College (an independent girls' school) seen to the right. Over the stile maintain direction along a line of oaks, but crossing a third stile bear half-right towards the far corner of meadowland, aiming well to the left of a church. The path then reaches a junction of roads by the entrance to Kent College (Grid ref: 626428).

Walk up the road to the church of St Peter, Pembury (3), passing through a fine old lychgate and taking the path out to the north-west corner of the churchyard. Bear left along a drive, then at the end of a sports field head to the right on a footpath going into woods. It soon veers leftwards through the woods, and emerges on a country lane. Bear right, come to a T junction and turn left as far as the entrance drive to Knowles Bank, which is on the right of the road. Walk along the drive, which eventually curves to the left of the large house and passes a number of stables. Come to the end of the drive near some converted oast houses and walk ahead on a grass track between paddocks, soon with long views over the Weald.

The way continues without diversion as far as the B2017 at Crockhurst Street. Turn left and follow this road for about ¹/₂ mile back to Tudeley Church, passing on the way a pub called The Carpenters At Tudeley.

Items of interest:

1: All Saints, Tudeley. A curious eighteenth-century red brick tower on a sandstone base gives this little church an unpretentious appearance. Clearly there was a church here long before the present medieval place of worship was built, for one was mentioned in the Domesday Book. What gives it appeal to visitors today, however, are the twelve Chagall windows. The first of these (a magnificent swirl of blue over the altar) was created in memory of Sarah d'Avigdor Goldsmid, who was drowned in 1963 in a sailing accident off Rye. Made in Rheims it was dedicated in 1967; seven others followed in 1974 and the final four were installed in 1985, the year of Marc Chagall's death.

2: St Thomas à Becket, Capel. The former village served by Capel's 900-year-old church was burnt down to prevent the spread of infection following the Black Death. The church is now maintained by the Redundant Churches Fund. Inside, the north wall of the nave reveals some faded   medieval wall paintings, uncovered in 1927.

3: Pembury Old Church. Dedicated to St Peter, the "old" church of Pembury stands some way from the main village, which is unseen from our walk. The nave dates from 1147; there's a squat Norman tower with a small shingle spire projecting from it, and table tombs in the churchyard. The "modern" church built to serve Pembury dates only from 1840 and is more than a mile away.

WALK 24: BRENCHLEY - MATFIELD - BRENCHLEY

Distance:	7 miles
Maps:	OS Pathfinder TQ 64/74 Paddock Wood & Staplehurst 1:25,000
	OS Landranger 188 Maidstone & The Weald of Kent 1:50,000
Start:	Brenchley church (Grid ref: 679417)
Access:	By signposted road off B2160 at Matfield, about 5¹/₂ miles north-east of Tunbridge Wells.
Parking:	Car park by the village playing field (Grid ref: 674418).
Refreshments:	Pubs in Brenchley and Matfield.

If one ever needed convincing that the Weald of Kent justifies the epithet of Garden of England, this walk should do it, for on this circuit a number of orchards are visited. There are also hop gardens and fields of soft fruit; a lush countryside of rich husbandry. Walkers are warned, however, that waymarking is poor, and due to various diversions having been made over the years, the actual route does not always correspond to rights of way indicated on the OS maps.

* * *

Brenchley Church (1) stands at the southern side of a three-way junction of roads at the eastern end of the village. A minor road (Windmill Hill) heads north of the triangle, and the walk begins on a surfaced path between walls down the side of the timber-framed Town Farm Cottage.

When the path makes a left-hand bend, go straight ahead, cross a stile and go down a sloping field towards a small woodland. From the foot of the slope climb uphill along the left-hand edge of the wood, and beyond it beside orchards as far as a narrow lane at Palmers Green. Turn right, soon passing through a gateway leading to Hononton Farm and walk along the drive between neat orchards. At the end of the drive turn right to pass the timber-framed farmhouse, and continue ahead on a track, again between orchards. Eventually reach a gap in the shelter-belt of trees alongside which you've been walking, and bear left beside another row of protective trees. On reaching the far bottom edge of the orchard turn right and wander ahead to reach a road (Grid ref: 684410).

Opposite stands a handsome timber-framed house with a pond in front. Bear right and almost immediately cross the road to a farm track. Just beyond some low buildings cross a stile on the left, then turn right to walk along the edge of a field. In the far corner come to a stile and a choice of paths. Continue ahead along the lower edge of a wood, rich in wood anemones and bluebells in season, soon passing alongside a long pond with more orchards stretching up the slope on the far side. Out of the woods the way continues ahead, then between fences with another pond on the right and a mass of broom on the left.

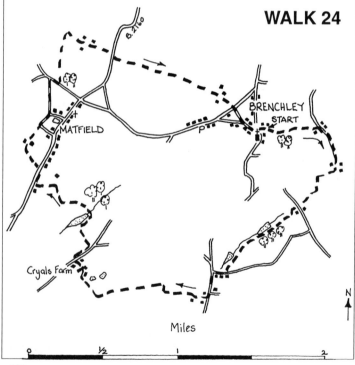

Come to Spout Lane, bear right and soon after reach a T junction. Turn left and walk uphill, near the top of which a lane cuts off left. Just beyond this junction head to the right on a driveway to pass a bungalow. A few paces after the bungalow a footbridge on the right leads over a ditch and into an orchard. Turn left along the edge, and at the far side go through a gap in the boundary hedge and continue straight ahead (another orchard). At the far side cross a stile, turn right, and about 30 yards later bear left along a broad grass divider between yet more orchards heading towards a field gate.

Through the gate walk directly ahead on a track which soon curves to the right, still among orchards, and leads to Cryals Farm. Stay on the tarmac drive that continues from the track, and when it forks in front of large packing sheds walk ahead (following one-way road signs) through one of the open sided sheds and eventually out to Cryals Road (Grid ref: 661404).

Cross the road, go over a stile into a field and immediately turn right. On coming to the far side bear left and a few paces later go through a gate onto a track. Walk down the track and at the bottom, just before a small lake, turn right over a stile and along a fence-enclosed path, at the end of which come to a crossing path. Bear left and pass beyond the end of the lake. The continuing path leads eventually to a concrete drive. Bear left to reach the B2160 beside Friars Mill. Turn right for about 300 yards until, just after passing the entrance to Friars, a stile is seen beside a field gate on the left of the road. Cross this and walk ahead over two small fields (the fences here might not be permanent), but in the middle of the third (large) field come to a crossing path and bear right towards an oast house.

Cross a stile in the hedge. A footpath leads to a drive just beyond the oast house and to the right of a converted barn. Along the drive come to Matfield (2) village green and continue along its left-hand side. When the green ends walk ahead still along a lane until reaching a road junction. Turn right, and in about 200 yards bear left into the edge of a small wood. A clear path leads through. Emerging, bear left for a few paces, then right alongside a hedge. In a second field views begin to open in the north where the Weald slopes to the Medway valley.

On reaching a farm track cross ahead and a few paces later turn right on a footpath that keeps left of a line of trees. This soon comes onto a drive leading to some converted oast houses. Follow the drive to the B2160 road, cross half-right to another drive (to White Barn Farm), soon heading between orchards. When it curves sharply left, leave the drive and go ahead, over a stile and along a series of orchards linked either by stiles or gaps in the hedgerows. Views left into the ever-expanding Weald are delightful.

Maintaining direction the way eventually leads through an orchard towards more oast houses. About 100 yards before them veer slightly right, then left to a drive beside a house. Walk down it, and when it joins a second drive bear right on a footpath which soon forks. The right-hand option slopes down through orchards to join the Brenchley road near the car park; the left-hand alternative leads to a junction of roads. Wandering down Holly Bank soon reach the heart of Brenchley by the war memorial not far from the church.

Items of interest:

1: Brenchley church. Approached along an avenue of well-clipped yew trees the church is about 600 years old, but was much restored in the Victorian nineteenth century; the Old Vicarage apparently dates from around 1320. The village street is full of charming houses and pubs and the group gathered round the triangle near the church makes an idyllic picture. This open triangle was formerly occupied by the village pound. Siegfried Sassoon lived nearby and wrote about the area in *The Weald of Youth*.

2: Matfield. Originally part of Brenchley parish this spacious village lines one of the largest greens in Kent. To the north of the village the seventeenth-century Crittenden House has a beautiful garden with two ponds and is occasionally open to the public.

WALK 25: LAMBERHURST - HOATHLY FARM - LAMBERHURST

Distance:	3$\frac{1}{2}$ miles
Maps:	OS Pathfinder TQ 63/73 Wadhurst, Cranbrook & Bewl Bridge Reservoir 1:25,000
	OS Landranger 188 Maidstone & The Weald of Kent 1:50,000

Start:	The Chequers Inn, Lamberhurst (Grid ref: 677363)
Access:	Lamberhurst is on the A21 about 6 miles south-east of Tunbridge Wells.
Parking:	Public car park behind The Chequers Inn.
Refreshments:	Pubs in Lamberhurst, none on route

The first of two short walks based on Lamberhurst, if combined with Walk 26 a figure-of-eight route amounting to 6¹/₂ miles could be achieved. However, both walks have much to commend them when taken individually. This particular route explores farmland to the west of the village with views towards Bayham Abbey and through the neat little valley drained by the River Teise, one of the major tributaries of the Medway, but seen here in its infancy. There are several attractive buildings on this walk, a beautiful garden, rolling hills of a Wealden ridge, orchards and vineyards, and the gentle charm of lowland countryside.

* * *

From the car park at the rear of The Chequers Inn bear right along the main street for a short distance, cross the River Teise and soon after turn left into Brewers Street. At the far end is a complex of industrial buildings; continue ahead on a track between fields for a little over ¹/₂ mile. The River Teise winds round on the left, and the track forks with one branch curving to cross it. Take the alternative route which goes ahead then veers right and forks again by some rough sheds. Climb the right-hand slope on a sunken track as far as the edge of Timberlog Wood, then turn left on a crossing path. Walk along the top edge of a field alongside the wood, with a fine view through the gentle valley of the Teise. Oast houses add interest to that view, as does the large grey building of distant Bayham Abbey (1).

At the far side pass into a second field through a gap, and walk across the slope to a stile and a plank footbridge in the opposite boundary. Now walk ahead along the right-hand edge of the next field. When the boundary cuts off to the right strike out across the centre of the field aiming half-left towards a group of oast houses seen a couple of fields away. The path leads to them, passes between the oasts and Hoathly Farm, onto a drive, then left to a country lane. Bear left for a short distance. Just beyond the entrance drive to a converted oast house turn left along a farm road (Grid ref: 656366).

This soon curves to cross the Teise, passes alongside a wood (masses of wild garlic in spring) then veers left. Continue to a large corrugated barn and walk along its right-hand side to enter a farmyard. Pass an oast house on the left, then bear right in front of a weatherboarded building. Continue along the drive as far as the B2169. Immediately on the left a lake may be seen in the midst of an exotic garden.

Bear left on the road, and shortly after passing a junction, turn left again through a gate and follow footpath signs uphill through a garden. Cross a drive and continue uphill, through a metal squeeze stile then left along a fence-enclosed path above a large house. Enter a field and cross half-left to the hilltop, then follow the field boundary to the right.

Walking ahead now Lamberhurst (2) shows snug in its hollow, while Goudhurst crowns a distant hill. A large number of oast houses punctuate the view. Come to a crossing track near farm buildings. Go downhill for a few paces on a concrete farm road, then break away to the right, up a few steps and emerge in an orchard with a vineyard to the right. Maintain direction and wander alongside a succession of orchards and vineyards with fine views ahead and behind.

When the farm drive curves to the right leave it and continue ahead, eventually descending some steps to a road. Before doing so pause to admire the splendid panorama of rich husbandry spread out behind, assured that Kent remains the Garden of England. On the road bear left and walk downhill into Lamberhurst.

Items of interest:

1: Bayham Abbey. Built on the right bank of the River Teise by Premonstratensian monks in the early thirteenth century, the abbey ruins stand skeleton-like and roofless in the care of English Heritage. The Bayham Abbey that is seen from our walk, however, is a gabled Victorian mansion on the north slope of the valley. While the ruined abbey is in Sussex, the mansion is in Kent.

2: Lamberhurst. Once a centre for the iron industry, Lamberhurst is now very much a village or orchards, hop gardens and vineyards; in fact it boasts England's largest vineyard producing white wines

From the lip of Wye Downs the village of Brook can be seen below *(Walk 35)*
This large field of oil-seed rape stretches to Lenhall Farm near Bishopsbourne *(Walk 36)*

The path that makes a rising traverse from Alkham to the woodland crown of the hills on the way to St Radigund's Abbey *(Walk 39 - A route)*
The coast path that leads from St Margaret's Bay to Kingsdown *(Walk 40)*

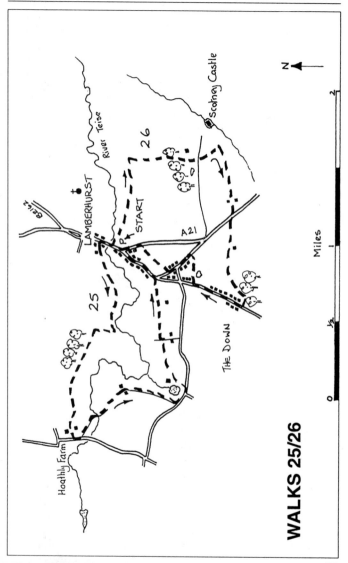

WALKS 25/26

from a grape of German origin. The church stands off a side road on the northern outskirts of the village, gazing over a delightful folding landscape. Dedicated to St Mary, it was built in the fourteenth century and has a Perpendicular tower with a shingle spire rising from it. A recent memorial window, installed in 1985, was designed by John Piper.

WALK: 26 LAMBERHURST - SCOTNEY CASTLE - THE DOWN - LAMBERHURST

Distance:	3 miles
Maps:	OS Pathfinder TQ 63/73 Wadhurst, Cranbrook & Bewl Bridge Reservoir 1:25,000
	OS Landranger 188 Maidstone & The Weald of Kent 1:50,000
Start:	The Chequers Inn, Lamberhurst (Grid ref: 677363)
Access:	Lamberhurst is on the A21 about 6 miles south-east of Tunbridge Wells.
Parking:	Public car park behind The Chequers Inn.
Refreshments:	Pubs in Lamberhurst.

Owned by the National Trust, Scotney Castle is a romantic ruin set in a small lake below a cascading garden of exotic trees and shrubs; the design of Edward Hussey who lived there in the nineteenth century. This short walk passes within a few paces of the entrance, and provides an ideal opportunity to make a visit. Elsewhere the walk presents other highlights. Before reaching Scotney, for example, a glorious vista of field, meadow, orchard, hop garden and vineyard is given, with Lamberhurst church and neighbouring Court Lodge drawing the eye from their prominent position north-east of the village. Later, a sweep of close-cropped parkland holds its own beauty. Finally, a close view of Lamberhurst is seen through a trellis of vineyards. A short walk it may be, but there's no shortage of interest.

*   *   *

Go through a gate at the back of the car park behind The Chequers Inn, enter a playing field and walk directly ahead. On the far side cross a stile and continue straight ahead over several sections of a golf course. (Take great care, mindful of flying golf balls.) Finally cross another stile into a field. Ahead is a concrete farm road.

Walk ahead across this narrow field to the concrete road and go directly uphill towards a clump of pine trees. On the way up the slope views to the left are splendid. Reach the pine trees, cross a stile on the right and follow the top boundary of a field to reach another stile on the far side. In a few places go through a gateway and maintain direction. Soon slope downhill on the left-hand side of a small woodland. Beyond this continue in the same direction to find another stile leading into the wood opposite.

A woodland path strikes ahead among trees and comes to the driveway leading to Scotney Castle (1) (Grid ref: 685354). If it is open and you plan to visit the Castle, turn left.

The walk now crosses the drive and enters a sweeping parkland through a gate. Go down the slope ahead (the Castle ruins may be seen among trees to the left), but shortly before reaching a stone bridge at the foot of the slope, turn right and follow a faint path which leads to a field gate and a stile. Over this walk on to reach a drive by a few buildings, beyond which is the busy A21 (Grid ref: 679351). Cross this road with great care and go ahead along the right-hand boundary of the field opposite. Midway along this field bear right through a gap, then resume direction towards Whiskett's Farm. Continue across the next field, and on reaching the far boundary go over a stile and a few paces later turn left on a footpath between woodland and the back of a row of houses.

Eventually come to a fence and bear right between bungalows, emerging onto the B2100 at The Down. Turn right and pass several houses, rising up a slope to a small woodland containing a pond. The first building after the woodland is Lamberhurst Surgery. Immediately after this bear right and walk along a tarmac drive. When this finishes go ahead on a footpath overlooking the pond. Come to The Brown Trout pub opposite some large converted oast houses, turn left and when the road forks continue directly ahead. About 80 yards later bear right on a concrete farm road. It leads alongside a vineyard overlooking Lamberhurst rooftops, the church on the slope ahead and Goudhurst seen far off to the right. When the drive makes a sharp bend to the left, go half-right on a footpath sloping downhill between vineyards.

At the time of writing there is a proposal to build a school near the foot of the slope. If this is approved the line of the path is likely to be rerouted; but in any case it is likely to lead (as now) onto the A21 a short stroll from the car park behind The Chequers.

Items of interest:

1: Scotney Castle. Standing on a small island in a moat created by the damming of the River Bewl (which flows into the Teise near Finchcocks below Goudhurst), most of the castle dates from the seventeenth century, but the single turret is of the fourteenth. It was built by Roger de Ashburnham during the Hundred Years' War, but was never tested in battle with the French. In the fifteenth century it was taken by the Darell family who lived there for 350 years. In 1778 Edward Hussey bought it from the debt-ridden Darells, and it was his grandson (another Edward) who in 1836 built an imposing Tudor-Jacobean style house at the top of the hill overlooking the castle and, with the help of Sawrey Gilpin, created a magnificent garden from the quarry out of which stone had been taken for his new home. He then aided the castle's "picturesque decay", producing the romantic image now enjoyed by thousands of visitors each year.

WALK 27: CRANBROOK - HOCKER EDGE - CRANBROOK COMMON - CRANBROOK

Distance:	6¹/₂ miles
Maps:	OS Pathfinder TQ 63/73 Wadhurst, Cranbrook & Bewl Bridge Reservoir 1:25,000
	OS Landranger 188 Maidstone & The Weald of Kent 1:50,000
Start:	Cranbrook church (Grid ref: 777362)
Access:	By way of the A229 Maidstone-Hastings road. Cranbrook lies south of the Goudhurst-Tenterden road, A262.
Parking:	Car park between the church and windmill (Grid ref: 778360).
Refreshments:	Pubs in Cranbrook.

Woodlands, streams and rolling Wealden acres provide landscape contrasts on this walk. Deep in the heart of the Weald Cranbrook owes it generously wide street, its airy church and fine houses to the days when the town became an important centre of clothmaking, thanks to weavers from Flanders lured there by Edward III in the fourteenth century. By-passed by main road, Cranbrook is most attractive with rows of white weatherboarded houses and a handsome smock mill standing on a brick base with its sweeps rising above the surrounding buildings. Seen from afar, the early nineteenth-century windmill makes a fine landmark. Surrounding the town gentle valleys have been scoured by innocent-looking streams. Hall houses built for yeoman farmers of a bygone age overlook some of these valleys, while converted mills that once took energy from the streams now command beautiful gardens, both tended and wild, that provide rich palettes of colour from spring until autumn.

* * *

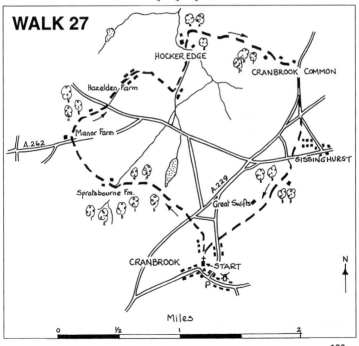

WALK 27

HOCKER EDGE

CRANBROOK COMMON

Hazelden Farm

A.262

Manor Farm

SISSINGHURST

Spratsbourne Fm.

A.229

Great Swifts

CRANBROOK

START

P

CRANBROOK

N

Miles

0   ½   1   2

Walk through the churchyard of St Dunstan's Parish Church to a playing field. Continue ahead beside a row of houses with the playing field on the right, and soon reach Cranbrook Primary School. Bear right on a footpath enclosed by a wooden fence and a hedge. The path swings left, and on coming to a meadow and a junction of paths, take that which goes half-left across the meadow. On the far side an enclosed footpath leads between houses and comes to the A229 (Grid ref: 775367). Cross with care and walk directly ahead along a drive (footpath sign to Flishinghurst). Soon join a footpath parallel with the drive; it slopes downhill among trees and alongside a woodland of silver birch with the paddocks of Angley House on the left.

The path eases uphill and comes to a junction. Continue straight ahead to enter Gravel Pit Wood. The path forks again. Once more continue straight ahead, ignoring the left-hand option. As the way progresses through the wood there are other alternatives, but each should be ignored in favour of this main trail which begins to descend among beech, birch and a few oak, continues over a crossing path and descends among conifers. Cross a footbridge over a stream with the lovely timber-framed Spratsbourne Farm seen through the trees. At a junction of paths turn right and walk alongside the farmhouse (Grid ref: 765371).

Walk ahead on the farm drive for $^{1}/_{2}$ mile to reach the A262. Cross with care to the entrance to Manor Farm, then bear right with a pond on the left. Cross a stile by a field gate and go ahead along a track leading to Dunley Wood. Do not enter the wood, but go through a small gate on the right, walk through a paddock to another gate at the far end and enter a patch of birchwood. The path is unclear on the ground, but the way goes forward to a small footbridge and a stile on the right near a boundary fence surrounding another paddock. Over the stile follow the edge of a coppice woodland, with the paddock to the left. Traces of footpath may be found as the way passes alongside a bungalow. Come to a crossing path, continue ahead and soon arrive at a narrow lane (Grid ref: 765382).

Directly ahead a drive leads to Hazelden Farm. Walk along it, through the farm with three oast houses on the left, to a small prefabricated cottage named Orchard View. Immediately after this turn right on a track alongside woods to open fields with big views over a valley formed by a tributary of the River Beult. Walk ahead along the right-hand side of a line of trees separating two fields, and eventually reach another narrow lane opposite a large Elizabethan house called Friezley. Turn left and walk up the lane.

Passing a few houses open countryside then spreads out near the top of a hill. The lane descends at Hocker Edge, passes a few more houses, then over a stream that plunges in a waterfall. On the left a complex of buildings includes Hocker Edge Oast, set in a scoop below the lane. About 30 yards beyond its driveway take a footpath climbing on the right through more woods. Out of the trees come to a meadow and walk up to its top right-hand corner (views to the north are fine). Cross a fence by a gateway, veer slightly right and follow a main path rising into Hilly Wood. It soon leads alongside a garden on the left, becomes a track and leaves the wood behind to enjoy more Wealden views. The track develops as an unmade drive, then a surfaced narrow road beside several houses, and eventually comes to the A229 at Cranbrook Common (Grid ref: 789386).

Turn right. In about 400 yards the road forks. Continue directly ahead on the minor road (B2083) signposted to Sissinghurst, and come to a staggered crossroads. Walk ahead for about 20 yards, then cross a stile into a field on the right. Follow the left-hand hedge, and in the opposite corner cross a fence (the stile was missing at the time of writing) by a large oak tree and continue ahead. A short distance along the field boundary veer left through a gap and follow a footpath along the bottom of gardens. Enter another field, maintain direction and cross a stile in the far left-hand corner onto the A262. Cross the road and bear right, then left on a private road leading to Buckhurst Farm.

The road curves left. Cross a stile on the right beside a field gate and walk downhill parallel with the right-hand boundary fence to find a stile at the bottom. This leads to a broad grass path cutting through woods, and after rising uphill comes to a crossing farm road. Walk directly ahead to pass below the grounds of Great Swifts (rhododendrons, azaleas, clematis and glorious specimen trees). Views include several oast houses and, in addition, Cranbrook windmill (1).

When the farm road ends a clear footpath continues from it.

Come to a road by some houses, cross straight ahead and walk along the left-hand edge of a playing field leading to Cranbrook churchyard.

Items of interest:

1: Cranbrook windmill. Built by James Humphrey in 1814 on behalf of Henry Dobell, Union Mill is one of the largest of its kind in England, and it towers over the houses of Stone Street. When Dobell's business failed just five years after taking over the mill, it was taken on by a partnership of his creditors, hence the name. By the early 1950s it had fallen into disrepair, but experts from Holland were employed to restore it. Once again the sweeps turn and barley is rolled by electrically driven machinery. The mill is open to the public at set times.

WALK 28: LINTON - WEIRTON PLACE- RIVER BEULT - LINTON

Distance:	8½ miles
Maps:	OS Pathfinder TQ 65/75 Maidstone, and TQ 64/74 Paddock Wood & Staplehurst 1:25,000
	OS Landranger 188 Maidstone & The Weald of Kent 1:50,000
Start:	St Nicholas church, Linton (Grid ref: 755502)
Access:	Via the A229 about 3½ miles south of Maidstone.
Parking:	Public car park immediately to the north of the church.
Refreshments:	Pubs in Linton, and at Stile Bridge.

Linton enjoys a sun-trap of a position on the southern slope of the greensand hills. Away from the road huge views overlook the Weald with the River Beult curling sedately at the foot of the slope, and the glint of small farm reservoirs breaking an expanse of orchards and fields of soft fruit. The Garden of England, as seen from the village, appears as one vast market garden. To the east stretch green swards of parkland, then orchards and more parklands with deer grazing. To the west there's a bewildering complexity of fruit trees; orchard after orchard, immaculately pruned and

Linton, one of the several small villages that overlook the Weald

regimentally set along the slanting hills. There are a few hop gardens too, and platts of cobnuts. But down at the foot of the slope the Weald has open meadows and fields heavy with wheat or oil seed rape. The River Beult divides this land and enables our circuit to sample the contrasts.

* * *

The walk begins by following the Greensand Way. It then drops to the Beult in the depths of the Weald for a lowland riverside section before returning to Linton through that orchard wonderland. In spring everywhere seems puffed with blossom, but following wet weather some parts of the walk may be heavy underfoot.

Walk through Linton churchyard heading east (away from the road), through a metal swing gate and into Linton Park (1) following Greensand Way markers. Cross a driveway and continue in the same direction, passing behind a ragstone house and over a narrow country road (Loddington Lane). Soon after passing a converted oast house views begin to open to the right.

The path maintains its eastward course among orchards and alongside fields of soft fruit, always with immense views to the

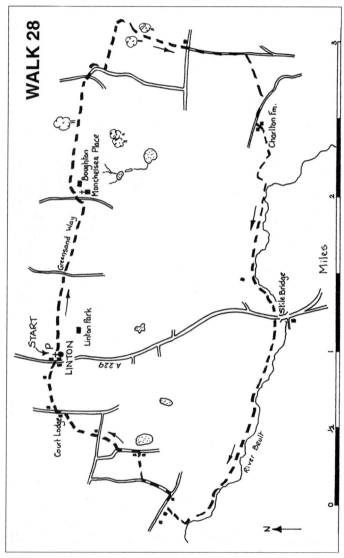

right. Then the stumpy tower of Boughton Monchelsea church is seen ahead, followed by the farm-like entrance to Boughton Monchelsea Place (2) next to it. The path swings left, just before reaching a road, then crosses the road and winds through a small coppice woodland. Out of the trees cross a meadow, then over a driveway and into a large field. Over this enter a second large field and on the far side cross a stile beside a pair of gates. Continue past Weirton Place and over its drive (swing gates either side) keep to the left of a fenced area of trees. Reaching a narrow road bear right (Grid ref: 784499).

Take the left-hand road at a junction soon after, follow the lane round a bend by a farm, and at the next bend opposite a house, go left through a gate into an orchard. Bear right and walk down the edge of the orchard, cross a stile at the bottom and turn left. Walk ahead between more orchards and over a stile descend steps to a sunken track, thought to be part of a Roman road that ran from Rochester to Bodiam in Sussex.

Bear right and walk down the track, leaving the Greensand Way which soon veers left. The track becomes yet more sunken and (at times) rather muddy. Eventually arrive at a junction of lanes at the foot of the slope beside a half-timbered cottage (Grid ref: 786489). Walk straight ahead along Forge Lane for almost $^1/_2$ mile, then leave it at a field gate on the right by a dilapidated corrugated building.

Go through the gate and walk across the field to a stile on the far side. Enter a second field and cross straight ahead to a ditch with a very awkward stile leading into a third field. Walking over this towards a farm, come to another stile and out to a lane. Bear right, walk past the entrance to Charlton Farm, then left over a stile and straight ahead through a small field. Wander between barns, then turn right and go through the left-hand of two field gates. Follow the right-hand hedgerow to the far end, then through a gateway into the next field. Bear right through the second of two field gates and follow the right-hand hedgerow round two sides of a large field to reach a small woodland by the River Beult. A stile leads into the woodland, and another on the right leads out to water meadows.

Follow the river westward for about a mile (stiles and footbridges aid the way). Come to the A229 at Stile Bridge (Grid ref: 759478). Should you be in need of refreshment there's a pub a few yards away to the left.

Cross the road and follow the continuing path on the right-hand side of the river for a further 1¹/₂ miles. On coming to a footbridge over the Beult leave the riverside, bear right and walk along a track between fields. When it curves left towards a farm go straight ahead on a footpath beside a small orchard to reach a driveway next to a house. Turn right, and right again on a road. Now take the first turning on the left; a very narrow lane heading north-east (Bonflower Lane).

After about 300 yards cross a stile on the right and walk uphill across a field, bear left round a small orchard, then right to go downhill onto another lane (Laceys Lane) between two houses opposite an attractive lake. Turn left and when the lane curves leftward go straight ahead through a gate into an orchard. Walk ahead between trees and reach yet another narrow lane opposite a row of white weatherboarded cottages. Continue uphill on a path to the left of the cottages, and at the far end of the orchard cross a stile, bear right up a slope to pass alongside some buildings, and reach Vanity Lane (Grid ref: 749501).

Turn left and follow a high hedge of cypress trees. When these end at a farm drive, bear right (signpost to Linton church) and walk along a metalled drive above a broad slope of fruit trees, until just past a lone pink house a flight of steps on the left lead to The Bull Inn almost opposite Linton church.

Items of interest:

1: Linton Park. The house, with its Corinthian columns, was built in the 1730s by Robert Mann on a magnificent site overlooking the Weald. Horace Walpole described it: "...like the citadel of Kent, the whole county its garden". The house was enlarged by Thomas Cubitt in the nineteenth century.

2: Boughton Monchelsea Place. Set beside the Church of St Peter, whose doorway must surely have one of the finest views in all Kent (and whose medieval lychgate is said to be the oldest in England), Boughton Place was built in 1567 from local ragstone, on the site of an earlier manor house. It is open to the public on set days during the summer.

WALK 29: ULCOMBE CHURCH - BOUGHTON MALHERBE - GRAFTY GREEN - ULCOMBE

Distance:	7 miles
Maps:	OS Pathfinder TQ 84/94 Headcorn & Charing, and TQ 85/95 Harrietsham 1:25,000
	OS Landranger 188 Maidstone & The Weald of Kent, and 189 Ashford & Romney Marsh 1:50,000
Start:	Ulcombe church (Grid ref: 847498)
Access:	The church is ¹/₂ mile north of Ulcombe on a minor road (signposted) running south from A20 ³/₄ mile east of Leeds Castle.
Parking:	Limited parking by the church - please avoid service times.
Refreshments:	Pubs in Grafty Green.

Magnificent panoramas over the Weald are on view during much of this walk, which follows a section of the Greensand Way eastwards, then returns through lush agricultural countryside below the greensand hills before rising again on their southern flank. Following the Greensand Way is straightforward, thanks to first-class waymarking, but once this route has been left behind footpaths are often unseen on the ground and, it has to be said, during field research some of the stiles were not in very good condition. However, don't let this dissuade you from tackling what is potentially one of the best of all walks in this book.

* * *

From the Norman church of All Saints, Ulcombe (1) cross the road heading east where the Greensand Way goes alongside a cottage, then down the right-hand side of a sloping meadow which is invariably wet from a number of springs that rise nearby. Enter and pass through a small woodland with a pond on the left, then go up a slope where broad views open to the right. A stile leads into another field and the way continues to a row of poplars. Walk along their left-hand side, then enter a meadow and go across to the far boundary and another stile. Do not cross this, but instead turn left and walk up to the top corner. Over a stile descend steps into an orchard, then head uphill to a narrow road (Grid ref: 857495).

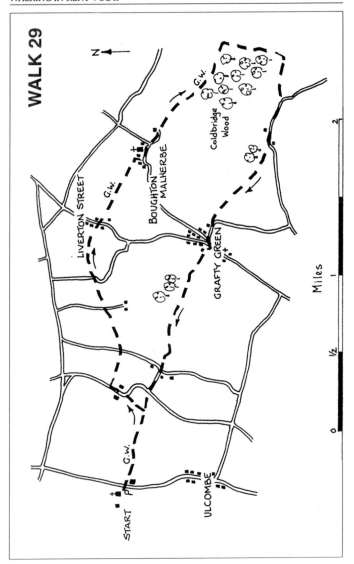

WALK 29

N

LIVERTON STREET

G.W.

BOUGHTON MALHERBE

G.W.

Coldbridge Wood

GRAFTY GREEN

START P

G.W.

ULCOMBE

Miles

0   ½   1   1½   2

Turn left along the road for about 350 yards, passing between Upper Hill Farm and Weald View Farm, then over a stile on the right walk across a hilltop field to a dividing line of trees. The path goes along their right-hand side to a very narrow lane and through a gap into the field ahead. Cross to the far left-hand corner and enter a woodland area of hazel coppice which, when in foliage, is like walking through a leafy tunnel.

On coming to a very narrow driveway (Grid ref: 866500) bear left, then right a few paces later on a continuing path along the edge of a platt of hazelnuts, then into an orchard of fruit trees. In the far corner a stile leads onto yet another narrow lane at a bend, and into more orchards to go half-left between rows of fruit trees. Passing through a gap in the opposite hedgerow the way now crosses a region of bushes and trees, then along an enclosed path at the bottom of gardens in Liverton Street.

Cross the road, go up some steps and ahead on the continuing footpath beside Churchill Cottage. This may be a little overgrown with nettles in spring and early summer, but there are snatched views between trees into the Weald. Come out of an enclosed section to a large field with vast uninterrupted views. Ahead is Boughton Place (2) with Boughton Malherbe Church (3) seen above farm buildings. The path enters the farmyard. Bear right through it, then left along a road to the church (Grid ref: 883495).

Beyond the church the road curves left with a minor lane dropping to the right. Go down this lane to enjoy a wonderful view that opens onto the Weald. The lane veers left towards The Old Rectory (4) overlooking a pond. Pass in front of the house, go through a field gate and walk directly ahead. Just beyond a small barn (seen on the left) cross a stile and walk across a large meadow veering a little to the right (occasional posts with Greensand Way markers). The panorama is magnificent. Another stile is found just to the left of a small copse. Cross over and continue ahead to pass to the right of Pope Hall Cottage. The way curves left and passes alongside the garden boundary.

Walk along the left-hand (northern) edge of Coldbridge Wood, and at its eastern end bear right on a bridleway/track. A few paces later the Greensand Way breaks away to the left. Ignore this and continue ahead along the rutted track. It edges Coldbridge Wood, and about 150 yards after the wood finishes, the track is crossed by a path. Bear right through a gap in the hedge and strike across a large field to its far left-hand corner to find a footbridge over a ditch with a stile into another field. Walk ahead half-left to the far side to a field gate by a large oak tree. Go onto a country road a short distance from Coldbridge Farm (5).

Turn right along the road for about ¹/₂ mile. When it curves sharply left by Roughets Wood head to the right along the edge of a field with the wood to the right and a small stream below. (At the time of writing there were no waymarks, stiles nor signs of footpath on this section.) Cross out of the field beyond the wood and continue ahead along the right-hand edge of a large field. On reaching a gateway on the right go through it, bear left and maintain direction. When the hedge makes a sharp right-hand turn, cross a stile and walk ahead along the left-hand edge of another field. Continue ahead through a gap into a final field and at last reach a gate leading onto Woodcock Lane (Grid ref: 875487).

Bear right, pass Ash Tree Farm and come to a junction of roads at Grafty Green. (There is a pub a short distance to the right; also Post Office Stores.) Turn left at a T junction and in a few yards go right on a narrow path by the side of an electricity sub-station, then beside a bungalow and ahead through its garden to wooden bars in the top hedge. Cross these, walk uphill half-right to a woodland, then bear left alongside it. At the field corner cross a stile and continue alongside the wood, but when it cuts back to the right walk ahead to another stile found by a large oak tree.

The way continues through a rough rectangular meadow. At the far side veer left through a gap, then maintain direction to the right, soon coming to a farm track rising uphill which leads to a junction of lanes. Walk directly ahead to pass a half-timbered cottage on the left, soon with more splendid views. Come to a T junction and cross to a footpath descending among trees. (Caution when wet.) Enter an old orchard and walk along its right-hand edge, then left at the far end for a few paces before crossing a stile on the right into a field. Cross to the far left corner, rejoining the outward Greensand Way. Retrace this outward route back to Ulcombe church.

Items of interest:

1: All Saints, Ulcombe. An attractive Norman church ¹/₂ mile from the village, it was built of Kentish ragstone and, according to legend, on the direct instructions of William the Conqueror. It has seen numerous additions during its long history, including a Tudor north chapel, fourteenth-century tower and medieval wall paintings. In the churchyard stands an enormous yew tree thought to be about 3000 years old.

2: Boughton Place. Overlooking the Weald in this tiny hamlet, Boughton Place is all that remains of a much larger Elizabethan mansion built for the Wotton family, one of whom (Sir Henry) was born there in 1568, became a diplomat in Venice and is remembered for having described an ambassador as an "honest man sent to lie abroad for the good of his country". Izaak Walton wrote Sir Henry's biography, in which he said of Boughton Malherbe that it has "the advantage of a large Prospect". Which is most certainly has.

3: St Nicholas, Boughton Malherbe. Another ragstone church, but much smaller than that at Ulcombe, it contains a number of brasses to members of the Wotton family of Boughton Place. The attractive Bell House next door was built as a school in 1848.

4: The Old Rectory. According to Alan Bignell in *The Kent Village Book*, one of the rooms in this large grey house is haunted by the ghost of a hunchback monk. Apparently one of the former rectors living there wanted to test the legend, and offered overnight lodging to passing tramps. None managed to spend more than a couple of hours in the room.

5: Coldbridge Farm. Set down in the Weald south-east of Boughton Malherbe, it occupies the site of a former fourteenth-century castle built by Fulk de Peyforer; earthworks and a surrounding ditch remain.

WALK 30: PLUCKLEY - LITTLE CHART - EGERTON - PLUCKLEY

Distance:	6¹/₂ miles
Maps:	OS Pathfinder TQ 84/94 Headcorn & Charing 1:25,000
	OS Landranger 189 Ashford & Romney Marsh 1:50,000
Start:	On the B2077 in Pluckley (Grid ref: 926455)
Access:	Via B2077 about 3 miles south-west of Charing. Pluckley railway station is 1¹/₂ miles south of the village.
Parking:	With discretion in the village.
Refreshments:	Pubs in Pluckley, Little Chart and Egerton.

A major part of this walk follows the Greensand Way on its linking of three villages in a circuit that enjoys wide vistas over a peaceful agricultural land. Each of the villages holds something of interest, while the countryside itself is most attractive with an array or orchards spilling blossoms in springtime.

* * *

In Pluckley's (1) main street linking Smarden with Charing, about 100 yards north of the Bethersden turn-off, a Greensand Way signpost directs the start of this walk into a playing field on the eastern side of the road. On the far side, about 20 yards from the right-hand corner, enter an orchard and walk ahead through it. The Greensand Way then leads through a series of orchards, passes alongside the beautiful garden of Sheerland Farm and crosses a farm drive. Soon after, come to a narrow lane. Cross it and continue ahead alongside a wall. Over a stile maintain direction along the left-hand edge of a field, with the large house of Surrenden seen off to the right and views of the North Downs to the left.

Enter another orchard and wander directly through it, then over a stile in a shelter belt of trees veer left round the edge of yet more orchards. On coming to the second boundary corner cross another stile and slant through a large field towards Little Chart church (2).

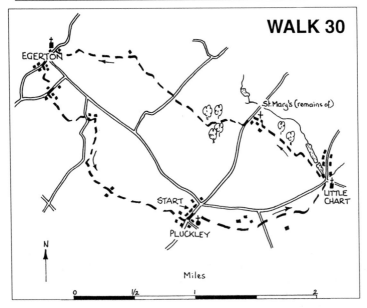

WALK 30

EGERTON

St. Mary's (remains of)

LITTLE
CHART

START

PLUCKLEY

N

Miles

0   ½   1   2

The path reaches a road just left of the church by The Swan Inn (Grid ref: 944459). Bear left (leaving the Greensand Way) and at a T junction cross directly ahead on a track leading into a field. A footpath edges the right-hand boundary from which it may be possible to see one of two mill ponds through trees on the right.

Bear left with the field edge, then turn right on the continuing footpath, soon joining a track alongside fields, woods and orchards. Come to farm buildings with a ruined church tower seen ahead. Now on a concrete farm road, take the right-hand option when it forks. It curves left towards a pair of oast houses. About 10 yards before them slant right on a footpath into the churchyard of St Mary's, whose shell of a tower remains a symbol of the medieval church destroyed by a flying bomb in World War II. Pass alongside the ruins and come to the B2077 once more (Grid ref: 934467). ·

Turn left to pass Chart Court and Chart Court Farm, beyond which the road curves slightly. Cross a stile on the right by a field gate and walk ahead along the edge of an orchard. Continue ahead into a second orchard and maintain direction. Bear left at the far corner and follow the boundary to Little Piper's Wood. A stile on the right gives access to the wood and a footpath goes through it (masses of bluebells and wild garlic in springtime).

Out of the wood bear right on a crossing track, from which there are fine long views to the North Downs. Eventually reach a very narrow lane (Grid ref: 924469). Turn right, then left on a continuing track which soon leads alongside a small wood and with views growing to the left; Egerton church is seen across the fields. Join a narrow lane just short of Iden Farm Cottage, with a dutch barn on the left. Leave the lane, pass alongside the barn and then slant across a large field towards Egerton church.

On the far side of the field come to a track and a junction of paths by a water tank. Bear half-right and walk down the track for about 250 yards, then enter an orchard by a gate on the left and walk through it. At a boundary corner turn right, and in about 100 yards cross a stile on the left. Bear half-right towards Egerton church, and crossing several stiles come to a house and go through a wooden gate on the right, then sharp left alongside houses to a rough drive. Turn right and come to the main street in Egerton (3) opposite the ragstone church (Grid ref: 908476).

Turn left, once more on the Greensand Way, and walk through the village. Immediately beyond The George Inn lovely Wealden views draw the eye with more than a hint of space. Just past the pub the village primary school is seen on the right, and opposite this the Greensand Way heads left along Elm Close. The footpath resumes behind the right-hand bungalow down the Close, and along the headland of a field to a narrow lane. Turn right for about 200 yards, then bear left into the entrance to Stone Hill Farm. Pass a converted oast house, then veer slightly right on a descending concrete farm road with more splendid views into the Weald ahead.

At the end of the concrete a footpath continues ahead tracing a natural hillside terrace curving left above Britcher Farm. Passing through gates or over stiles the way leads through a small woodland and into a sloping meadow. Far ahead may be seen the spire of Pluckley church. Keep to the left-hand edge with a high, tree-covered bank above, and come to another stile. Over this climb a short flight of steps to a country lane, then wander downhill with yet more wide views ahead. The lane bends to the right. Turn left on a rough drive by Greenhill House. At the entrance to Greenhill Farm go through a gate on the right and wander down a slope slightly left; over a ditch bear right to a stile. Now walk ahead along the right-hand edge of a large field divided halfway by a fence. On the far side come to a gate and a stile giving access to a meadow with a brick-walled barn in it.

Cross the stile, bear right and come to a track. A few paces later cross another stile on the left and walk along the left headland of a field. On reaching the far corner go over a plank footbridge and a stile on the left, then half-right across a field corner to yet another stile. The way now strikes directly across a field towards Elvey Farm. Walk ahead through the farmyard (Grid ref: 915457). Despite several paths and a bridleway merging here, there were no waymarks at all when this walk was surveyed.

Passing the farm and a converted oast house go through a gate and ahead along the right-hand edge of a meadow. In the far corner go through another gate, and after about 30 yards veer slightly right, then left to maintain direction with a ditch on the left. Soon pass through another gate on the left, but continue in the same direction along the right-hand field boundary. When this cuts back to the right maintain direction uphill aiming just left of Pluckley church. More gates and stiles lead the route uphill before veering right to an unsurfaced driveway between houses. Come to the B2077 in Pluckley and bear left to complete the circuit.

Items of interest:

1: Pluckley. Said to be one of the most haunted villages in England, it is attractively set among orchards on a brow of the greensand hills. The church of St Nicholas dates from the thirteenth century and is built of Kentish ragstone with a broach spire that makes an effective landmark. Near the church a small square is overlooked by the Black Horse public house whose arched, white-painted windows give the appearance of quizzical eyebrows. These are typical of the village, for Sir Edward Cholmeley Dering, a local squire, had the windows of every house in Pluckley altered to this design in the nineteenth century.

2: Little Chart. The same Dering-style windows are found in a number of houses in Little Chart, a village built on the banks of the Great Stour, which at this point is a modest stream that used to power Ford Mill. The church of St Mary was built in 1955 to replace the original St Mary's (visited on this walk) that was destroyed in World War II. Built of brick, the neo-Gothic present-day church looks curiously out of place, its tower resembling a water tower.

3: Egerton. A neat village crowded at a T junction of minor roads with fine views south over a sudden slope that drops to the low meadowlands of the Weald. Crowning the village the grey Perpendicular church tower is topped by a small turret; a feature common to a number of churches in the Weald of Kent.

WALK 31: DODDINGTON - EASTLING - YEWHEDGES - DODDINGTON

Distance:	6 miles
Maps:	OS Pathfinder TQ 85/95 Harrietsham 1:25,000
	OS Landranger 178 Thames Estuary 1:50,000
Start:	Doddington church (Grid ref: 940575)
Access:	By narrow road (signposted) south-east from B2163 1½ miles above Hollingbourne, or by minor road (signposted) north from Lenham.
Parking:	With discretion in the village.
Refreshments:	Pubs in Doddington, Newnham and Eastling.

Apart from a distant drone of traffic on the M2 at the start of the walk, the majority of countryside explored in this isolated corner of the North Downs enjoys a refreshing peace. It's a land of soft curves and well-moulded shallow valleys; a land of woods and hedgerows, of open spaces too, and orchards and grazing sheep. Three small villages and two tiny hamlets settle these downland furrows. The villages (Doddington, Newnham and Eastling) have fine churches worth sitting quietly in. They also have pubs offering refreshment, and at Newnham the remains of a former encampment of ancient Britons now, alas, spoilt by the dumping of rubbish. Each of the villages has a manor of sorts. In addition there are handsome timbered houses and attractive flint cottages typical of the downs. But it is a spacious countryside that beckons. Songbirds rejoice among the woods and pheasants pace their fringe. Step softly and absorb all it has to offer.

* * *

Between Doddington church (1) and the former vicarage a short drive leads to a footpath that enters the parkland of Doddington Place. Through a swing gate bear half-left and cross the parkland (Doddington Place is seen to the right) to the far corner, there to enter Sharsted Wood (2). The continuing path leads to a woodland track and maintains direction to Sharsted Court (3) (Grid ref: 951582).

Sharsted Court is a formidable red-brick and flint building partially hidden behind flint walls and an ornate iron gateway. Some interesting topiary is seen within the grounds. A drive veers to the right, then forks.

Take the right branch which joins a narrow lane, at first with Sharsted Wood to the right and a timber yard on the left. The lane

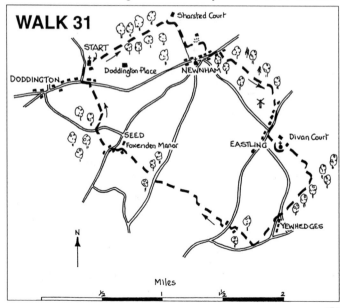

then goes alongside an orchard before sloping downhill towards Newnham (4). At the end of the orchard cross a stile on the left and walk along the top edge of a sloping meadow, near the end of which there's a small fenced area marked as Motte and Bailey on the OS Pathfinder map; the site of a defensive camp used by a tribe of ancient Britons (Grid ref: 955578). A few paces later wander downhill and come to the main street in Newnham. (Those in need of refreshment will find a pub a few paces to the right.)

To continue the walk turn left along the road for about 200 yards, then just before a playing field turn right on a track between houses. From the track take a footpath entering Lady's Wood, then rise up a slope within it. The path veers left and emerges from trees at a small open meadow. Walk up its right-hand edge and re-enter woods on the far side. Ignore alternatives and continue ahead on a footpath which hugs a fence, veers right and slopes downhill. Come to a stile and an enclosed footpath heading back to the right. Ignore it and instead take that which goes half-left ahead. Leave the woods and continue through a narrow woodland shaw, with a modern power-generating windmill seen to the right.

The shaw broadens to a small wood. On drawing level with the windmill look for a footpath forking to the right and follow it between ugly stout corrugated "fences" - a hideous "tunnel" section of path that eventually disgorges by Glebe Cottages on the edge of Eastling (Grid ref: 965570). Turn right on the road towards the centre of the village. About 40 yards beyond the lane which cuts off to Newnham, bear left on a tarmac footpath leading to Eastling church (5). (Note: a pub is found a short distance further along the road.)

Next to Eastling church stands Divan Court, a white-painted house with flint-walled barns nearby. The path curves round to the right of the churchyard wall, crosses a footbridge over a deep ditch behind it, then bears left. About 50 yards later turn right and walk directly across a field to gain another belt of woodland. The path goes straight through these woods, veers right then left to cross a narrow inner valley and reaches a larger wood on the far side. Come to a crossing path and bear right, then follow this clear path through stands of hazel coppice for almost $1/2$ mile before coming to a narrow junction of country lanes (Grid ref: 965557).

Cross directly ahead and go along the left-hand edge of the field opposite, walking parallel with a lane which rises to the few cottages of Yewhedges. The valley-bed field is long and narrow with woods rising on either side. At the far end veer left to join a narrow lane, then bear right. Pass a track on the left, and in a few paces veer right on a path rising among woods. At the head of the slope cross a stile into a hilltop field and walk ahead, aiming to the right of a flint-walled house (Skiltons). With the garden fence on the left come to a boundary corner, cross a stile into the garden, bear right through a single gate and walk through a small orchard towards a row of white cottages. Come to a narrow lane, turn left, and just beyond the last of the cottages find a stile in the right-hand hedgerow by an electricity pole. Enter a field, and a few paces later cross another stile into the right-hand field and turn left alongside a fence.

When the fence breaks away left, strike ahead half-right across the large open field, soon to join a grass track which divides this from the next field. Continue along the track to the far side (Doddington Place may be seen far-off). Bear right on a narrow lane for a few paces, then go left on a broad path through yet another woodland strip leading to an open field. Cross slightly to the right and walk up the opposite slope with a dividing hedge and line of trees to the left. A continuing track between fields passes to the right of a bungalow, swings left then right and joins another narrow road beside Foxenden Manor in the hamlet of Seed (Grid ref: 944565).

Turn left. The lane curves right towards Sandhurst Farm. Just before the farm take a drive on the right by the side of Seed Bungalow, then cross a stile directly ahead into a small paddock. A second stile leads into a field. Cross this half-right and enter woods on the far side by a stile found about 100 yards from the end of the field. The path rises through the woods and in a few paces comes onto another country lane. Bear right, then left on a continuing path through open coppice woodland, soon emerging to a large field with a grand view directly ahead to Doddington church and the large gabled Doddington Place.

Walk ahead along the right-hand edge of the field for about 40 yards to reach a crossing path. Turn left and cross the field aiming towards the church. Come onto the Doddington-Newnham road through a gateway, bear left towards the village, then take the minor road on the right signposted to Doddington church.

Items of interest:

1: Doddington church. Unique in its dedication to the Beheading of St John the Baptist, the flint-walled Norman church dates from about 1100. Its curious, white-painted tower looks rather like a squat water tower, and replaces an earlier one destroyed by lightning in 1650.

2: Sharsted Wood. An extensive woodland owned by the Forestry Commission; a mixture of evergreen and deciduous trees.

3: Sharsted Court. This large and impressive house with a Queen Anne frontage, was built in 1711.

4: Newnham. This small village at a junction of several minor roads was occupied long before the church was built, for on the hillside to the north early Britons made a fortified encampment. It is thought that the church was provided by Hugh de Newenham in the twelfth century. De Newenham also built the original manor house, now known as Champion Court.

5: Eastling church. (See p117) The Domesday Survey of 1086 suggests that Eastling was then a prosperous community. The original Saxon church was replaced by the present flint-walled Norman church of St Mary. An enormous yew tree crowds the doorway.

WALK 32: TENTERDEN - ST MICHAELS - TENTERDEN

Distance:	6 miles
Maps:	OS Pathfinder TQ 83/93 Tenterden 1:25,000
	OS Landranger 189 Ashford & Romney Marsh 1:50,000
Start:	Tenterden Town Railway Station (Grid ref: 882336)
Access:	Via Station Road north of Tenterden High Street. Tenterden is served by bus from Maidstone, Headcorn, Canterbury and Ashford.

| Parking: | Public car park near the station (Grid ref: 883334). |
| Refreshments: | None on route, but pubs in St Michaels and Tenterden. Tenterden also has cafes. |

South of Tenterden the Weald folds into the levels of Romney Marsh, but to the north, the countryside explored on this walk, an easy rolling land of meadow, field and woodland stretches broad and promising; a surprisingly remote patch of country with far distant views and an overwhelming sense of peace its main ingredients. There are plenty of small ponds too, and pleasant streams. And although this is mainly a sheep-grazing corner of the county, there are hop gardens along the way, and assorted crops to paint patterns and contrasting shades among those distance views.

* * *

Begin by the station operated by the Kent and East Sussex Railway (1). On the northern side of the level crossing a field is used as the station car park, but is for passengers only. (A public car park is provided about 150 yards south of the station near the town's museum.)

At the entrance to the station car park there are two footpaths; take that which follows the left-hand boundary. It soon veers slightly left to leave the car park, parallels a drive then comes to a field gate and a stile. Over this bear right along the edge of a sloping meadow, at the foot of which a plank footbridge gives access to a second undulating meadow. To maintain direction the way crosses a damp, boggy area on a railway sleeper by some willows, then up a slope veering away from the right-hand boundary. (A large pond may be seen off to the right.) At the top of the slope pass a small pond by some mature oak trees and go ahead alongside the garden boundary of a large house. Go through a swing gate, walk ahead beside a wall and come to a narrow lane.

Cross the lane, go over a stile and keep ahead on a footpath signposted to Millponds. Enter another meadow sloping downhill and follow the left-hand boundary. (Pleasant rolling views dotted with oast houses.) At the foot of the slope a sturdy footbridge has been provided over a stream. The walk continues ahead a few paces, then up a short, steep grass embankment. Turn left along the top, and when it ends bear right, cross a stile by a field gate and walk ahead into a lovely shallow valley with a stream meandering

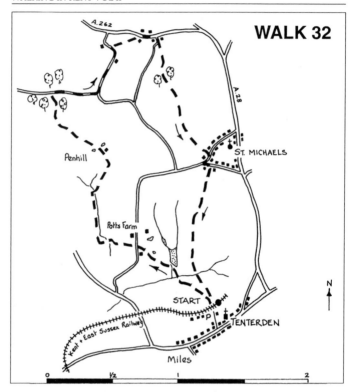

WALK 32

A.262

A.28

St. Michaels

Penhill

Potts Farm

START

Kent + East Sussex Railway

TENTERDEN

Miles

N

0   ½   1   2

through and Pott's Wood on the far side.

Eventually enter a belt of woodland (Grid ref: 867348) marked Breeches Pond on the 1:25,000 map, and turn right on a crossing path. It soon veers left, rises uphill, then forks by a marker post. Bear left. Not a public right of way, the path is used by courtesy of the landowner; a broad trail that provides a pleasant stretch of woodland walking. Come to the edge of the woods where a stile leads out to a field. Do not cross the stile, but instead bear left on a descending path guided by yellow paint marks on trees. Cross a stream on a footbridge, leave the woods and wander across the bottom right-hand corner of a meadow to another stile, over which go up a slope that may be somewhat tangled with nettles and brambles (a stick could be handy here).

The path reaches the farm of Penhill (Grid ref: 870354). Bear left on the farm drive and continue ahead alongside a pond (on the right). Over a stile enter a large field and go along its left-hand boundary, beyond which there are fine views. At the top corner enter the next field ahead and continue in the same direction. On the far side a stile is found a few paces from the corner. Over this cut across a sloping meadow towards its top left-hand corner. Another stile a few paces to the right of the corner leads into a woodland coppice with a clear path leading through. On coming to a fork take the left-hand option; eventually emerge onto a narrow country lane and turn right (Grid ref: 864361).

The land is most pleasant as it passes first through woods, then fields and hop gardens before coming to a T junction. Bear left. The lane continues its leafy way; in spring when the may blossom is shaken by a breeze it's like walking on a carpet of confetti. Just before reaching Haffenden Farm a gap in the trees provides another lovely view off to the right. The lane curves left. Near the entrance to a farm called Bugglesden a footpath sign directs our walk over a stile on the right and into a field. Cross this half-right to a field gate in the opposite boundary. Through the gate walk towards a bungalow on the far side of the field where a small gate leads into the garden. Go ahead on the left-hand side of a cypress hedge, and out to the A262 (Grid ref: 874367).

Bear right for about 130 yards, then turn down a very narrow lane by Questover Farm. In a few yards the lane makes a sharp right-hand bend. Leave it here, cross a stile next to a gate and walk ahead through a series of untidy small fields linked by stiles. This part of the walk is dotted with a number of small ponds.

Soon walk alongside a strip of woodland, then enter the wood. Veer left (a marker post directs the way), and emerge in the corner of a rectangular meadow. Cross diagonally to the bottom left-hand corner. Go through a woodland shaw with a fence on the left, cross a stream and over another stile into an open meadow. Walk directly ahead to the far left-hand corner and find a footbridge and yet another stile under a large oak tree. Continue ahead on the left-hand boundary of two fields, over a stile and down a short slope to cross a stream, then up the right-hand edge of the next field. The path veers right over a stile and ahead through a long woodland shaw. Emerge into a short, narrow meadow and continue towards houses. Go into the garden of a house called Dering Lands, and walk down the drive to a road in the village of St Michaels (Grid ref: 883354).

Turn right, come to a junction of roads and bear left for about 150 yards. At a public footpath sign turn right on a track which leads along the edge of several fields with views ahead to Tenterden church (2). The track finally ends but the way continues ahead on the right-hand edge of a field, at the far side of which a stile leads into the next field. Follow the left-hand boundary of two fields, go down a slope and over a footbridge. The path continues towards the church, and the final stile of the walk is a "clapper stile" erected by Tenterden Footpath Group in 1993, providing access to the field used as the station car park.

Items of interest:

1: Kent and East Sussex Railway. Operated by a group of steam railway enthusiasts, the one-time branch line, which was closed by British Rail in 1961, was reopened in 1974 to run initially from Tenterden to Rolvenden. Since then the line has been extended as far as Northiam in East Sussex, and with plans to push the route to Bodiam and Robertsbridge in order to connect with Network South-East trains. The railway has a collection of 16 steam engines, with seven in working order. Kent and East Sussex Railway operates daily throughout the summer months, and on selected days the rest of the year. Enquiries to K&ESR, Tenterden Town Station, Tenterden TN30 6HE (01580 765155) (See Walk 33).

2: Tenterden church. St Mildred's church has a magnificent fifteenth-century pinnacled tower that is seen for miles around. It is said that as a warning of the approach of the Spanish Armada (when Tenterden was much nearer the sea than it is today) a beacon was lit from the top of the tower. The chancel is of the thirteenth century, the nave from the fourteenth, but a lot of rebuilding and refurbishment went on during Victoria's reign. The peal of bells is considered one of the finest in the south.

WALK 33: TENTERDEN (WITTERSHAM ROAD) -
SMALLHYTHE - TENTERDEN

Distance:	6 miles
Maps:	OS Pathfinder TQ 83/93 Tenterden and TQ 82/92 Rye 1:25,000
	OS Landranger 189 Ashford & Romney Marsh 1:50,000
Start:	Wittersham Road Railway Station (K&ES Railway) (Grid ref: 866287)
Access:	By Kent and East Sussex Railway from Tenterden Town.
Parking:	Tenterden Town Railway Station (Grid ref: 882336)..
Refreshments:	None on route.

By using the Kent and East Sussex Railway, this rather novel and enjoyable walk can be achieved from Wittersham Road back to Tenterden. It begins among low-lying farmland that once formed part of the seabed between Smallhythe (south of Tenterden) and the Isle of Oxney on Romney Marsh. Then it rises among vineyards and goes through a valley with a man-made lake and woodlands flush with wild flowers, before heading across open fields to Tenterden.

Note: The Kent and East Sussex Railway operates daily from June to September, but runs a limited service at other times of the year. For details telephone 01580 765155 (recorded message: 01580 762943) or write to: K&ESR, Tenterden Town Station, Tenterden TN30 6HE.

* * *

Buy a one-way ticket to Wittersham Road Station, a journey of about 20 minutes. On leaving the station bear left on a country road and go over the level crossing. In about 300 yards reach Maytham Farm where there are two options.

Route A: On the left of the road a footpath crosses two fields before emerging on a grass path near a broad drainage channel near Potman's Heath (Grid ref: 871282).

Route B: Continue along the road for about ½ mile, passing a waterworks building and rounding a left-hand bend. About 30

On land that was once sea, a footpath follows the drainage channel of Reading Sewer

yards before reaching a cottage, go through a double field gate on the left and along a line of pollarded willows. The path soon reaches a crossing track and the broad drainage channel mentioned above (Grid ref: 871282).

Routes A and B having combined, continue directly ahead, now on a grass path between trees, and reach a bridge crossing the Newmill Channel, a major tributary of the River Rother. Over the bridge bear right and enter a large open field by a pumping station. Cross the field towards the left-hand end of a line of trees. Low-lying one-time marshland rises to modest hills on the left with the gentle mound of the Isle of Oxney to the right.

Come to another major drainage channel with the unfortunate name of Reading Sewer. Bear left and wander along its left-hand bank, soon coming to a second pumping station (a corrugated building). Continue ahead, now on a track, but when it crosses a bridge to the road, walk on for another 100 yards to a minor drainage ditch. Enter a new field and cross to a line of willows. On reaching them keep ahead with a ditch on the right. In the field

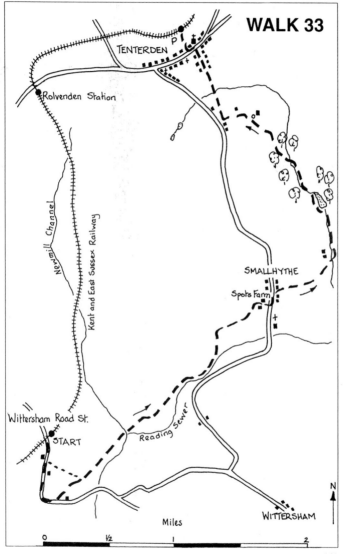

WALK 33

TENTERDEN

Rolvenden Station

Newmill Channel

Kent and East Sussex Railway

SMALLHYTHE

Spots Farm

Wittersham Road St.

START

Reading Sewer

Miles

WITTERSHAM

N

0   ½   1   2

corner go over a stile and cross a track near a red-brick, tile-hung house. Enter the field opposite and bear half-right, making a line towards a collection of farm buildings seen on a hill several fields away. A plank footbridge leads into a second field which is crossed to the far left-hand corner. Over a stile walk along a track between vineyards to Spots Farm. (Tenterden Vineyards; herb garden, vineyards and winery; open daily Easter-Christmas.) Veer right alongside the farm buildings and come to a road in Smallhythe (1). (Note: About 150 yards downhill is the Ellen Terry Memorial Museum - owned by the National Trust.)

Turn left for about 100 yards to a telephone kiosk on the right beside a double field gate. Through the gate aim half-left across a small paddock (in effect crossing the lower end of a garden) towards a pair of oast houses seen several fields away. Over a stile continue down a slope to another field gate. Through this bear half-right towards the far corner of a field, through another gate and along the right-hand boundary of a large field divided in two by a wire fence. On the far side cross a footbridge over a ditch and enter another field. Cross to the right of the oast houses and, gaining the brow of the field, aim towards an angle of boundary hedge. Continue ahead with the hedge on the left, and in the field corner go through a gate into a smaller field near the oasts. A stile is crossed in the opposite fence. Pass below a small orchard and ahead along the left-hand boundary of a field, now entering a gentle valley whose walling hillsides rise to woodland.

At the far corner cross another stile and continue towards a track. Cross this about 10 yards to the right of a bend, and continue along the left headland of another field. Come to a crossing track and go ahead, now up a grass-covered embankment overlooking a lake. Walk along its left-hand side. Below runs a stream, its banks a drift of wood anemones and primroses in early spring and, later, wild garlic. Along the lake's edge bulrushes quiver in the breeze, while on the opposite side a number of dead trees stand naked in the water. There's a heronry in the woods rising from it.

Beyond the lake the path continues beside the stream, soon with a woodland on the left. Several stiles are crossed, then the way veers left through a narrowing of the valley and rises over a shoulder of hillside. Sloping down again come to a sturdy footbridge. Ignore it and continue, now winding through a tight little valley (celandine, primroses, wood anemones, bluebells and wild garlic in abundance) to enter the woods. Cross a plank footbridge and, shortly after, a more sturdy footbridge, then go up a slope to the edge of a field. Turn left, go round a curve and bear right to a group of trees enclosing a small hollow.

Walk along the left-hand side of the trees and over the field beyond, cross a stile and aim half-left towards Belcot Farm. In the far corner cross a stile to the left of a pond, continue diagonally over the next field to a farm drive (Grid ref: 890325). Bear left to the B2082 road. Turn right through a gate and walk along a tarmac path that leads directly to Tenterden (2). Turn left in the High Street, then right down Station Road.

Items of interest:

1: Smallhythe. This hamlet down on the edge of Romney Marsh was once the port for Tenterden when much of Romney Marsh was covered by the tides. The heavily timbered Ellen Terry Museum, now many miles from the sea, was originally built for the harbour master in 1480. Nearby is the Priest's House, another fine half-timbered building next door to a small brick-built church.

2: Tenterden. The town grew to prosperity through the wool trade when Edward III brought Flemish clothmasters to Kent in 1331, but it also had the advantage of its own port down at Smallhythe. In 1449 Tenterden became a limb of Rye, a Corporate Member of the Confederation of Cinque Ports. Today it has lost the sea and its wool trade - though not its sheep. But the town still retains its air of prosperity and the High Street is one of the most picturesque in Kent with a lively assortment of attractive buildings facing one another across a broad, tree-lined thoroughfare.

East Kent

Every year hundreds of thousands of travellers pour into and out of Britain by way of East Kent. The M2, A2 and M20, not forgetting British Rail's rattle boxes, funnel all these comings and goings down comparatively narrow corridors and leave vast tracts of glorious countryside to a jealously guarded peace. Within half a dozen miles of Canterbury, Dover or Ashford the walker can amble in harmony with woodland birds, with rabbit and hare and hedgehog. Deer step lightly, as do fox and badger. There are orchids to clothe the slopes in springtime, and beautiful clear streams with watercress beds sidling through valleys where you'll have to strain your ears for sound of an internal combustion engine.

There are big views too. Long vistas that take in green hills and shimmering far-off seascapes. And clifftops bronzed with gorse.

Here the North Downs come down to the sea where they are abruptly carved by the tides. The White Cliffs of Dover extend north-east and south-west. Beneath them the gruesome Channel Tunnel and all that leads to it has scarred forever a once-majestic land. Stand on Sugarloaf Hill or Castle Hill above Cheriton; find your way to where Frogholt, Newington and Peene have been sacrificed to "progress" - and bite on your anger. Then go inland on any of the walks outlined in this section and revel in the uncluttered loveliness of a more gentle Kent - and know that some things are too precious to lose.

The northern "thumb" of East Kent is Thanet. Once a true island when the Wantsum Channel was a waterway busy with shipping between Reculver and Sandwich, Thanet looks to the sea, but has its back to low, extensive fields of cabbages. Yet to south and west hills rise barely detected as the shoulders of the downs. The continuing downs. The North Downs that have made such a long determined curve round the fringes of the Weald. All along their multi-mile scarp the North Downs have provided viewpoints of splendour and opportunities for some very fine walks. But where they project across East Kent, these same downs reach heights of perfection.

164

Above Wye, along the very lip of the land where the North Downs Way picks its route with considered care, an immense panorama floods the senses. To right and left as far as the eye can see a plunge of turf forms a link between earth and heaven. But there's the distant sea too, little more than a hint when the light is clear. And the low-lying Weald filling every available space; and Romney Marsh levelled between the downs and the sea.

Within the downs indented coombes and vales slumber as havens of lost gentility, unguessed by travellers dedicated to modes of transport that exceed a sedate three miles an hour. Those who know the trails and trackways carry passports to a lost world.

Invaders from past millennia trod these valleys and the downs and left a few relics of their culture. But it is the tread of Christianity that remains most evident. Canterbury is unchallenged in architectural splendour. Barfreston's south doorway is a treasure worth seeking, St Radigund's Abbey leaves you guessing as to its former elegance. And almost every village (and lost village too) stubs the landscape with its tower or spire, many of which have stood against the winds since Norman times.

The Great Stour is the major river of East Kent. Rising north-west of Ashford between the greensand hills and the downs themselves, it then curves through the town and sweeps roughly north-eastwards below Wye and on to Chartham before cutting through Canterbury and, joined by the Little Stour, twists round to Sandwich and the dunes of Pegwell Bay. Though not a great river, it's a waterway of character. A 38-mile walk has been devised through its valley between Ashford and Sandwich where some charming historic countryside may be explored.

The ubiquitous Romans made their presence felt along the Stour's valley, and the alignment of their roads has been mimicked by the highways engineers of every age since. Going from A to B in a straight line may be the aim of those in a hurry or with conquest in mind. But we who enjoy walking for the way in which our footpaths unlock the secrets of the countryside, will be well content with the meandering course of many of the trails that invite through East Kent.

* * *

EAST KENT COUNTRY PARKS AND OPEN SPACES:

1:   Kings Wood, Challock: A vast mixed woodland of about 1400 acres largely contained by a triangle of roads north of Ashford. The North Downs Way runs along its eastern edge.

2:   Denge and Penny Pot Woods, Chartham: About 120 acres of sweet chestnut coppice. Reached by way of Shalmsford Street or Chartham off the A28.

3:   Larkey Valley Wood, Chartham: 105 acres of ancient broadleafed woodland. Approached from either Chartham or Thanington.

4:   Perry Wood and Selling Wood: 150 acres of woodland. Plenty of footpath access; about 2 miles north-west of Chilham, between Selling and Shottenden.

5:   Church Wood, Blean: An extensive area of ancient woodland in the care of a consortium of conservation bodies, local authorities and a private landowner. Footpaths and trackways; west of Canterbury. Car park reached by way of Rough Common Road.

6:   Clowes Wood, Whitstable: Situated to the east of the Canterbury-Whitstable road, about 580 acres of mixed woodland. Picnic site, walks. Car park reached by way of the Chesterfield-Tyler Hill road.

7:   Reculver Country Park: A coastal site of 90 acres, with wildlife, geological and archaeological interest. Interpretation Centre, guided walks. Car park at Reculver Towers, east of Herne Bay.

8:   Grove Ferry Picnic Site, Upstreet: About 11 acres of riverside meadows by the Great Stour.

9:   Pegwell Bay Picnic Site: The estuary of the Stour at Pegwell Bay is where St Augustine landed in 597. The Picnic Site covers 70 acres of coastal grassland. Bird-watching, excellent views, public toilets. Access near Cliffs End on A256.

10: Bockhill Farm and The Leas, St Margaret's Bay: Adjoining clifftop areas with fine coastal views. (See Walk 40)

11: Langdon Cliffs, Dover: Between Dover and St Margaret's, another splendid clifftop site with footpath access to further stretches of coastline.

12: The Warren, Folkestone: About 350 acres of cliff and scrubland to the north-east of Folkestone. Visitor Centre, footpaths, access to beach; car parking by East Cliff Pavilion.

13: West Wood, Lyminge: Beside the B2068 about 9 miles south of Canterbury, nearly 450 acres of woodland. Picnic site, footpaths.

WALK 34: WYE - BOUGHTON ALUPH - BOUGHTON LEES - WYE

Distance:	6½ miles
Maps:	OS Pathfinder TR 04/14 Ashford & Lyminge 1:25,000
	OS Landranger 189 Ashford & Romney Marsh 1:50,000
Start:	Wye church (Grid ref: 054469)
Access:	Wye lies 1½ miles east of the A28 Ashford-Canterbury road. It also has a railway station on the Ashford-Canterbury line.
Parking:	Car park (signposted) near the church (Grid ref: 053468).
Refreshments:	Pubs in Wye and Boughton Lees.

Wye has grown up on the right bank of the Great Stour, a modest river that in the past managed to carve a trench through the North Downs. These downs curve in an embrace around the town to north, east and west. Yet Wye, better known today for being home to the agricultural college of London University, overlooks flat, low-lying land with big field systems stretching either side of the river. This walk explores that low-lying farmland, then teases at the downs above Boughton Aluph, thereby gaining a broad impression of the Stour's valley with all its agricultural intensity backed by the distant wall of the continuing downs. Part of the North Downs Way is adopted by our route.

* * *

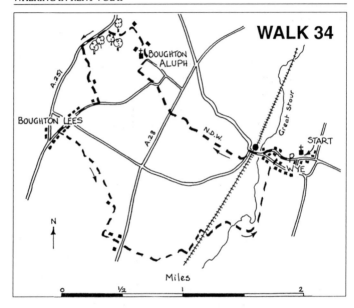

From the church walk down Churchfield Way heading west towards the railway station. Bear right at a T junction and cross the Great Stour by The Tickled Trout pub. Beyond the railway station turn left into Harville Road. After about 100 yards bear right on the North Downs Way which cuts straight across a field and by way of a stile into another. The footpath is clearly marked across this farmland, with the ridge of the North Downs making an obvious wall off to the right. Approaching Perry Court Farm the way leads alongside fields of soft fruit, vines and orchards, then through orchards to the Canterbury road (Grid ref: 037474).

Cross with care and take the footpath opposite (no longer North Downs Way) aiming directly towards Boughton Aluph church. On the far side of the field come onto a very narrow lane and turn left. In a few paces the lane curves in front of a tile-hung house. Now cross a stile into a field on the right, and bear left to find another stile in the left-hand corner. Over this walk across to a third stile leading into a narrow field in front of All Saints Church (1). In the far right-hand corner, between the church and a house, come to a driveway and turn left.

Walk along the drive serving Boughton Court, and veer right towards an oast house. Just to the left of the oast go through a gate and up a field to pass along the left-hand side of a white house. In a few paces the track/drive forks. Bear left. Views are fine looking down to the Stour Valley. Pass through a small woodland and come onto the A251 beside Kingswood Hill Lodge (Grid ref: 029484).

Turn left with great care along this road. After about 350 yards take to a bridleway heading left alongside the wood, beyond which the way becomes a sunken track between trees with views over a massed acreage of orchards. Eventually reach a very narrow lane and continue ahead. At a T junction turn right into The Pilgrims Way (also shared with the North Downs Way), which leads into Boughton Lees. Continue ahead at a crossroads, now with a large triangular village green on the right. (Those in need of refreshment will find a pub here.)

About two-thirds of the way along the green turn left beside Hobday Cottage (footpath sign). Past Pilgrim Cottage go over a stile and enter a field. The footpath leads through two adjoining fields, then through a gap in a hedgerow with farm buildings off to the left. Bear right along the boundary, then veer left and walk across to the opposite hedgerow corner to find a footbridge among trees leading into a large field. The way cuts diagonally across to the buildings of Park Barn Farm seen on the far side. Come to a concrete drive by the farm and walk along it a short distance, but just beyond the last house bear right, cross a stile into the next large field and walk straight ahead, aiming about 30 yards to the right of more farm buildings. Come to another concrete farm road and bear left to reach the A28 by Wilmington Farm (Grid ref: 031458).

Bear right for a few paces, then cross the road with care onto a farm track between fields. After about 500 yards a stream approaches from the right. At this point follow a footpath heading half-left; it leads to a footbridge over a narrow stream. Over this continue directly ahead towards the railway line. Turn left alongside the fence and in the far corner bear right across the railway. Go over a stile on the left, then half-right through a field towards a bridge seen ahead spanning the Great Stour. A stile in a wire fence gives access to the bridge which, at the time of writing, was badly in need of repair. On the east side of the river walk ahead, slightly left, to a footbridge crossing a minor stream. Bear half-left and follow the waymarked path across several fields back to Wye.

The town is entered between a sewage works and a school playing field, then to a road by the Village Hall. Turn right for a few paces, then bear left on a tarmac footpath between houses. This leads directly to Churchfield Way. Turn right and soon reach the church.

Items of interest:

1: All Saints, Boughton Aluph. Before the Normans came Bocton (as it was then named) had a Saxon church, seven and a half farms *(sulings)* and two mills. In 1210 the manor was taken by Aluphus of Boctune. It is thought that Aluphus began the present church to replace the earlier Saxon place of worship, and by its size it is obvious that the local congregation was then much greater than now, but was probably severely depleted by the Black Death. In September 1940 incendiary bombs badly damaged the tower. The weather and death-watch beetle further added to its deterioration. However, much has been restored, and although it is no long used for regular worship, All Saints remains an interesting building worth visiting. When we called there was a notice requesting the door be kept shut to prevent sheep getting in!

WALK 35: WYE - WYE DOWNS - COLD BLOW - WYE

Distance:	5½ miles
Maps:	OS Pathfinder TR 04/14 Ashford & Lyminge 1:25,000
	OS Landranger 189 Ashford & Romney Marsh 1:50,000
Start:	Wye church (Grid ref: 054469)
Access:	Wye lies 1½ miles east of the Ashford-Canterbury road (A28), Wye also has a railway station on the Ashford-Canterbury line.
Parking:	Car park (signposted) near the church (Grid ref: 053468).
Refreshments:	None on route, pubs in Wye.

Not only does the Wye Downs escarpment provide magnificent views over the Stour Valley and distant Romney Marsh, the nature reserve there protects as fine a chalk grassland as may be found anywhere in the county. Orchards, cowslips and butterflies adorn the slope; rabbits burrow in the scoops and hollows while skylarks and kestrels hover overhead. The North Downs Way makes a traverse of this glorious escarpment, while on bright spring and summer weekends families gather to enjoy a breath of fresh air with the county laid out below for inspection. This walk enjoys that panorama too, then descends steeply to the foot of the downs for a return to Wye by gentle fields and woodland shaws in marked contrast to that which has just been experienced.

*   *   *

Enter Wye (1) churchyard and take the path which branches right (North Downs Way). At the far side continue beside allotments and college buildings, then cross a narrow road and walk ahead along

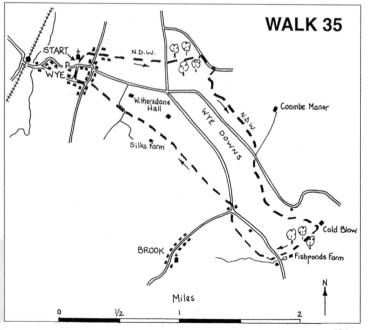

a drive to pass greenhouses. The drive becomes a stony track heading for the North Downs. About two-thirds of the way along it the Stour Valley Walk (2) branches off to the left; our route continues ahead, crosses a narrow lane and soon reaches the foot of the downs. Before entering trees, pause to admire the view over the Stour Valley.

Still on the North Downs Way climb the slope among trees. At the top emerge onto a very narrow lane with beautiful views ahead into a splendid steep valley. Bear right for about 300 yards, then cross a stile on the right and come to the lip of the downs with a spectacular view. Cross a stile and bear left, soon to wander above the (unseen) memorial crown cut in the steep scarp face by students of Wye College in 1902 to celebrate the coronation of Edward VII (Grid ref: 072466).

Continue along the scarp edge, cross one or two pitted areas, and eventually come to a field gate near the junction of a very narrow lane and the Wye-Hastingleigh road at the head of another superb inner downland valley. Bear right on the lane and cross the road to enter the wooded section of Wye Downs Nature Reserve (3), still on the North Downs Way. The path goes through the wooded area, curves left and then wanders over close-cropped open downland with those fabulous views again off to the right.

Eventually cross a stile and continue ahead, now with a wire fence on the left and the woods of Newgate Scrubs to the right. The path is led by a fence near kennels; it curves left, then right, and crosses a stile to a hilltop field. Follow the left-hand boundary and come to a field gate and then a track near the barns of Cold Blow Farm (Grid ref: 086448). Leave the North Downs Way here, turn right and when the track forks in a few paces go straight ahead, downhill among trees on a bridleway.

Descend between banks of cowslips and, at the foot of the slope, pass alongside Fishponds Farm to reach the Pilgrims Way. Cross the lane, go over a stile into a field where a second stile is found just ahead. Over this cross a brook and bear right through a field. A series of stiles linked by traces of footpath lead alongside the brook, then through trees to a large open field. Follow the right-hand boundary, but when it cuts back to the right continue ahead, slightly left, to find yet another stile in the opposite boundary. The way leads along the edge of a vineyard, then into a field, on the far side of which go over a track and across towards a house called Pickersdane at a junction of lanes (Grid ref: 074450).

The left-hand lane goes to Brook (4); Amage Road ahead goes to Wye. Walk ahead along this road for about 60 yards, then over a stile on the left and cross a field to the far corner. The footpath continues along the boundary of several fields, passes Silks Farm and on a track that leads to a narrow lane near Withersdane Hall - part of Wye Agricultural College. When the lane curves sharply to the right, continue ahead alongside a tall beech hedge and beyond playing fields to a residential street that comes to a crossing road. Bear left, and soon turn right into Church Street leading to Wye Parish Church.

Items of interest:

1: Wye. A very old town, it was known to the Romans, Saxons and Normans. There was a mill at the time of the Domesday Survey, and there's a mill on the Stour today. The church of St Martin and St Gregory has a curious squat tower; the original steeple was struck by lightning in 1572 and the rest of the tower collapsed just over a hundred years later wrecking both transepts and the chancel. Wye College was founded by John Kempe in 1447 as a college of priests. Kempe, incidentally, was a local man made good, becoming in turn Lord Chancellor to Henry VI, Bishop of Rochester, Chichester and London, and Archbishop of York and Canterbury. As Lambarde said, he was "...the childe of a poore husband man in Wye". In the eighteenth century Kempe's college became a grammar school, but was disbanded in 1893 and turned into an agricultural college.

2: Stour Valley Walk. Promoted by Kent County Council in conjunction with the Stour Valley Society, this is a 38-mile linear walk leading from Ashford to Sandwich. Clearly waymarked, KCC has produced an attractive guidebook to it.

3: Wye Downs Nature Reserve. Established in 1961, it covers 250 acres of downland on the steep face of the escarpment. Among its many wild flowers, 17 species of orchid have been recorded here. The dry valley known as the Devil's Kneadingtrough is a feature of the slope.

4: Brook. About 3 miles from the town Wye College's agricultural museum is housed in a large fourteenth-century barn in the village, with smaller items exhibited in an oast house.

WALK 36: BRIDGE - BISHOPSBOURNE - BRIDGE

Distance:	4¹/₂ miles
Maps:	OS Pathfinder TR 05/15 Canterbury & Chilham 1:25,000
	OS Landranger 179 Canterbury & East Kent 1:50,000
Start:	Bridge Parish Church (Grid ref: 184542)
Access:	By minor road (signposted) off A2 south-east of Canterbury. The church is in the High Street.
Parking:	With discretion in the village.
Refreshments:	Pubs in Bridge and Bishopsbourne. Bridge also has restaurants.

The busy A2 London to Dover road used to pass right through Bridge, but following a spate of accidents villagers took action to force the highways authority to build a bypass. During the 1960s and early 70s a series of sit-down protests was organised, effectively blocking the road and causing huge tailbacks on one of the most important trunk routes of southern England. After 14 years the protests bore fruit, and today Bridge receives mostly local traffic and is a much more pleasant place to visit. It nestles in the valley of the Nail Bourne stream with gentle hills rising on either side, and cropped parkland, large fields, woods and orchards clothing the slopes. Less than 3 miles away Canterbury is effectively hidden from view. Along the valley to the south-east several other small villages and hamlets, linked by charming lanes that meander through the leafy countryside, make this a most attractive corner to explore. Bishopsbourne is one of these villages and is included on this walk.

* * *

South of the parish church a minor lane breaks off from the High Street, and leads to Bishopsbourne. There is neither signpost nor nameboard. About 50 yards along the lane cross a stile on the left into a corner of Bourne Park. Two footpaths are signposted, but

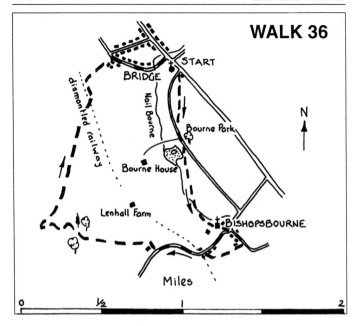

WALK 36

START

BRIDGE

Nail Bourne

dismantled railway

Bourne Park

Bourne House

N

Lenhall Farm

BISHOPSBOURNE

Miles

0 ½ 1 2

neither has any real evidence on the ground. Take the right-hand route, which effectively parallels the lane but some way from it. Ahead can be seen a small fence-enclosed woodland. Pass along its left-hand edge; beyond it a belt of trees leads to a larger woodland (Warren Plantation). A short distance along this belt of trees cross a stile into it and follow a footpath through. Come onto the lane near the entrance gates to Bourne House, and about 40 yards beyond cross a stile on the right. Bear half-left to pass the end of some trees bordering a lake (Grid ref: 185534).

Continue towards Bishopsbourne (1) church seen ½ mile away. Wandering across this parkland meadow the elegant Bourne House may be seen off to the right. Cross a stile in a wire fence dividing the parkland, then a few paces later go over a footbridge and continue ahead, still towards the church. Another bridge (a concrete one this time to carry farm vehicles) crosses the course of the Nail Bourne stream, which reputedly flows once every seven years. Shortly after

175

The lychgate in Bishopsbourne churchyard provides access to the village

this enter Bishopsbourne churchyard by a stile in the left-hand end of the boundary wall.

Go out through the lychgate to a junction of minor roads. Unless refreshment is needed, or you're uninterested in making a brief visit to the village, turn right along the country road to shorten the walk by ½ mile or so.

The full walk continues directly ahead (signpost to Kingston and Barham) along the village street. Immediately after The Mermaid pub turn right on a narrow drive passing some flint cottages and one or two other houses. The drive ends and a footpath continues between hedges, soon becomes a sunken trail, then reaches a stile into a meadow. On the far side will be seen several houses. Cross to the right-hand side of the left-most house and there join the country road coming from the church (Grid ref: 186524). Turn left and cross what used to be a railway line. The remains of Bishopsbourne station can be seen below and to the right of the bridge.

The road curves right between open fields, then forks at a left-hand bend. Keep left and on reaching a line of trees on the right take a footpath alongside them, with Lenhall Farm and its three unusual oast houses seen across the field. Partially obscured by the trees are one or two cottages. Bear left when the trees end. The path forks. Ignore that which heads off to the right and continue beside the boundary hedge. When it cuts back to the left walk ahead through the middle of the large field heading west.

Come to a crossing track. The map shows a path continuing across the next section of field to the left-hand edge of some pine trees. In effect there may be no footpath on the ground, and it may be preferable to follow the track round to the left, then right. This leads to the same point as the path.

At the edge of the pine trees (Grid ref: 174525) the route of the footpath meets that of the track, goes ahead through trees and continues towards a corrugated barn. Beyond this enter an orchard and bear left, still on the track. Within the orchard follow a shelter belt of trees going off to the right. At the end of these turn left for about 100 yards. A track curves right; at this corner cross a stile on the right into an adjacent orchard and walk along the right-hand edge - in effect back-tracking.

Cross a second stile into another large orchard and maintain direction, then over yet another stile continue along the edge of a field with pleasant views over a lovely rolling countryside. Eventually cross a bridge over the dismantled railway and come to a crossing track. Turn left and walk along it (Bridge church spire seen off to the right), to a row of houses. Just past these bear right on a lane which leads for about $1/3$ mile to a ford of the Nail Bourne stream, then curves left to the main road in Bridge.

Items of interest:

1: Bishopsbourne. This tiny village set in rural seclusion was once home to writers Joseph Conrad, Ford Madox Ford and Jocelyn Brooks. In an earlier age theologian Richard Hooker (died 1600) spent the last years of his life as rector here; he has a statuette by the pulpit. The church has a stumpy flint tower and a Burne-Jones window in the south chapel. Next to the church the handsome Court House surveys sheep-grazed meadows, while south of the village stands Charlton Park, a Tudor manor with Georgian additions, often visited by George IV.

WALK 37: ELHAM - DREAL'S FARM - ELHAM

Distance:	4 miles
Maps:	OS Pathfinder TR 04/14 Ashford & Lyminge 1:25,000
	OS Landranger 179 Canterbury & East Kent 1:50,000
Start:	Elham Parish Church (Grid ref: 177438)
Access:	On B2065 2 miles north-east of Lyminge.
Parking:	In the market square by the church.
Refreshments:	None on route, but pubs in Elham.

Elham and its valley count among the loveliest of their kind in East Kent; the village with its assortment of timber-framed or tile-hung houses, the valley with its gracious views, its sweeping downland slopes and its intermittent stream. It's a large village with an interesting High Street, one or two side streets lined with wonderful old buildings, and the market square tucked away beside the church. And it makes an excellent base for a number of first-class walks. This and the following route are merely two that are highly recommended. Others may be imagined by the tracery of dotted lines scored across the OS map.

* * *

The first walk from the market square in Elham (1) leads down Duck Street beside the church of St Mary the Virgin. At the foot of the slope bear left on a footpath alongside the Nail Bourne stream (2). On reaching the far side of the field bear right along its boundary. It curves briefly to the left. Cross a stile by a telegraph pole into the next field and walk ahead to a country lane. Bear right for a few paces, then left between houses. Go ahead through a small field and when the hedge boundary cuts back to the right, continue across the next field, now slightly to the right. The valley opens ahead, shallow, green and gentle, with woods marking the tops of several hills.

Go through a gate into a narrow meadow alongside a fence on the left, with a row of beech trees above to the right. Keeping to the lower edge of the meadow follow the boundary as it curves to the right and come to a stile. Over this wander ahead along the left-hand edge of a sloping meadow. Just before the hedge cuts off to the left, climb the fairly steep hillside on the right. Make for a point midway between the end of a wood on the right, and the left-hand boundary. (Splendid views into the valley.) Cross a stile beside a gate and walk along the right headland of a hilltop field towards a barn. At the end of the field bear left, then right, and come to a very narrow lane near Oxroad Farm (Grid ref: 192455). Turn right, pass a house and go into the field on the left. Walk through the middle, aiming half-right to a boundary corner. Cross another stile, go over the end bay of a smaller field and come to another lane (Grid ref: 194453).

Turn left for a few paces, then right over yet another stile into a large field. Bear half-right through it, and on the far side find a gate by Dreal's Farm. Through the gate and beyond a small pond on the right, veer slightly to the left to pass near a bungalow and join another country road. Turn right. In 50 yards go through a gate on the right into another large field. Cross towards the far left-hand corner where the path comes out near a junction of lanes (Grid ref: 190443).

Walk ahead for a few paces across a triangle formed by the lane junction, then bear left. Immediately beyond a house called Sherwood cross a stile on the right and walk ahead along the field boundary, soon to enjoy lovely views through a coombe of hillside. On the far side cross yet another stile and go half-right over a hilltop field with Elham coming into view in the valley ahead. The boundary hedge makes a kink, in which there will be found one more stile. Cross over and follow the lower boundary of another meadow. Halfway along it cuts down to the right, with a stile in the bottom corner. Over this walk through a large field and on the far side go through a gate by the Nail Bourne stream. Bear half-left across a meadow with Elham church seen ahead. Come to a drive which leads to the market square, entered beside The King's Arms.

Items of interest:

1: Elham. Pronounced "Eelam" the village is noted for its timber-framed buildings, one of the finest being Abbot's Fireside Hotel in the High Street, said to date from about 1480. Always an inn, the Duke of Wellington used it as his East Kent base during the Napoleonic Wars. The village had a thriving Monday market from the thirteenth century, but this died out in the nineteenth century.

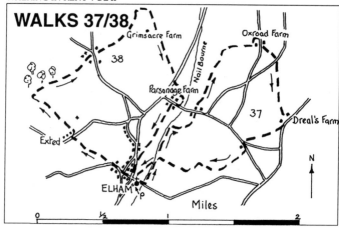

The market square today makes an attractive car park overlooked by the church, whose sturdy-looking tower is topped by a grey lead spire.

2: The Nail Bourne stream. Flowing intermittently through the valley, the Nail Bourne marks the beginnings of the Little Stour. In some summers it dries completely. Legend has it that St Augustine caused it to flow again after a particularly severe drought, but his actions so upset the pagan gods that they immediately sent forth a violent storm to block its flow again. Augustine then sought God's help in arranging for it to flow once every seven years. The stream, however, maintains its own schedule.

WALK 38: ELHAM - GRIMSACRE FARM - ELHAM

Distance:	3¾ miles
Maps:	OS Pathfinder TR 04/14 Ashford & Lyminge 1:25,000
	OS Landranger 179 Canterbury & East Kent 1:50,000
Start:	Elham Parish Church (Grid ref: 177438)
Access:	On B2065 2 miles north-east of Lyminge.
Parking:	In the market square by the church.
Refreshments:	None on route, but pubs in Elham.

Walk 37 explored the downs above and to the east of Elham's valley. This route looks to countryside north and west of the village. It's every bit as peaceful as that of the former, and consists of gentle coombes and minor valleys moulded from the downs themselves. On the crest of the downs the way leads through a small woodland, across open meadows and fields, and a curious region of buckled meadowland. Walkers should be forewarned, however, that a short but very steep slope needs to be tackled on the second half of the route, making for an energetic, if brief, pull.

* * *

From the market square walk along St Mary's Road to the High Street. Cross directly ahead and continue up a narrow street to the left of Abbot's Fireside Hotel (1). Turn left at a T junction beside Elham Manor, another splendid timber-framed building, and shortly after bear right into a lane rising uphill. At the top of the hill the lane curves left. Leave it here and go directly ahead, cross a stile and descend into a pleasant inner valley. Continue in the same direction across the corner of a second field. On gaining the left-hand boundary walk uphill on a narrow trail that soon becomes a sunken track beneath overhanging trees and leads to a narrow country road opposite three bungalows at Exted (Grid ref: 168443).

Turn right, but in a few paces cross a stile on the left, then wander over a hilltop meadow parallel with the left-hand hedge. Continue through a second meadow with the buildings of Exted Farm seen to the right. Halfway along cross a stile on the left, and maintain direction towards Clavertye Wood. Approaching the wood in the last field veer slightly left away from the right-hand boundary. Over a stile come to a crossing track (Grid ref: 163447) and turn right.

Follow the track on the edge of the wood, then alongside fields of soft fruit, to reach a junction of lanes by Upper Park Gate Farm. Cross both lanes to find a footpath sign among trees directing the way into a cottage garden. Veer right before the cottage, leave the garden by a small field gate and go ahead through a narrow meadow. On the far side cross a stile with a fine view into a tight little valley below to the right. Continue along the upper edge of a sloping meadow. In the far boundary find a field gate and another stile. Continue alongside the left-hand boundary of the next meadow, passing a buckled area just to the right. In the far left-hand corner go over a stile into a large field. Turn right immediately beside a wire fence to another stile leading back into the last meadow. Wander downhill half-left to yet another stile. Continue through a field to its bottom corner, well to the left of Grimsacre Farm seen in the valley ahead, and over a farm track.

Now comes a short but very steep, strenuous ascent of the slope directly ahead. At the top cross a stile, go over a hillside shoulder following the line of a fence, and wander ahead to the bottom right-hand corner of a field, just to the right of a shed. Go through a gate and along the bottom edge of a sloping meadow. The boundary makes an elbow bend, at which point maintain direction to reach a field gate leading onto the main valley road (Grid ref: 182450). Cross to a stile in the opposite hedgerow, and over this walk across to the far right-hand field corner near the buildings of Parsonage Farm (2). (The way through the farm was not waymarked during research; walkers will no doubt mingle with visitors on the farm trail.)

Enter the farm grounds by way of a stile. Continue ahead, slightly left, to wind among fences. Go through a field gate, turn right and walk through a meadow towards a stile seen to the left of a white cottage. Turn right on a lane and soon come to the farm entrance. Bear left, and walk ahead between dutch barns on a track. Just beyond the barns veer left through a gate, then continue on the right-hand edge of a long meadow with Elham church seen ahead. At the far end cross a stile and go along the right-hand edge of the next field, but before reaching the end cross a stile on the right and aim towards a field gate. This leads onto a track alongside gardens. Bear right on a road, then left in Elham High Street. About 200 yards later St Mary's Road leads to the market square.

Items of interest:

1: Abbot's Fireside Hotel. This splendid old building facing onto the High Street dates from 1480 and boasts some startling carvings on the beams, and on a huge lintel over the fireplace. Tradition has it that the future Charles II hid there in his flight from Roundhead troops in 1651, and during the Napoleonic Wars the Duke of Wellington used the inn as his headquarters.

2: Parsonage Farm. On the outskirts of Elham, Parsonage Farm has been turned into a Rural Heritage Centre open to the public (closed Mondays, except Bank Holidays). There is a museum of farming implements, a farm trail and a miniature railway.

WALK 39: ALKHAM - ST RADIGUND'S ABBEY - EWELL MINNIS - ALKHAM

Distance:	4¹/₂ miles (A route), 5¹/₂ miles (B route)
Maps:	OS Pathfinder TR 24/34 Ashford & Lyminge 1:25,000
	OS Landranger 179 Canterbury & East Kent 1:50,000
Start:	Alkham Playing Field (Grid ref: 256424)
Access:	On B2060 about 4 miles west of Dover. The Playing Field is by crossroads near the church.
Parking:	By the Playing Field, reached by minor road south of the crossroads (Grid ref: 256423).
Refreshments:	Pubs in Alkham and Ewell Minnis.

The B2060 provides an alternative cross-country route between Dover and Folkestone and passes through a charming valley carved out of the downs. Midway through this valley, on a kink in the road, Alkham snuggles around its church with the downs rising tree-clad behind. The church was built by monks of St Radigund's Abbey early in the thirteenth century, while the Abbey itself, or what remains of it, is found on the crest of the downs east of the village. Following the Reformation, Henry VIII had much of the Abbey pulled down and the stone removed to the coast for the construction of Sandgate Castle, but that which remains is worth a visit. This walk does just that by a choice of routes. The shorter and more direct way goes through woods on the downland slope, then across open meadows. The longer option is fine so long as there is no moto-cross event taking place at Poulton Farm, for the path crosses a dirt-track course! The two routes converge at the Abbey Farm, wander through woods, drop into the valley and climb out again on the northern side before visiting the hamlet of Ewell Minnis, then through a nature reserve and descending back to Alkham.

* * *

Route A: The Shorter Route (Alkham - St Radigund's Abbey)
Begin at the junction of B2060 with that of the minor road signposted to Hougham and Capel. A footpath sign directs the way to the far left-hand corner of the village playing field. Cross a footbridge over a ditch in the corner, then bear left on a footpath enclosed between a cypress hedge and a high wooden fence. This leads to a driveway,

which in turn leads to a narrow road. When it curves left go straight ahead on a surfaced bridleway. Passing a house the way continues, now unmade, curves slightly to the right and slants uphill with pleasant views along the valley.

The trail rises at a regular gradient before entering woods. Come to a T junction of bridleways and bear right, still within the woods, but soon leave them to continue ahead between fields guided by hedgerows. The bridleway goes alongside Oak Wood, then reaches a country road. Turn right and 100 yards later cross a stile on the left. Walk along the right-hand edge of a field, enter a second, smaller field, and continue to St Radigund's Abbey Farm, coming to a farm drive beside a pond (Grid ref: 274419). At this point the way is joined by Route B.

Route B: The Longer Option (Alkham - St Radigund's Abbey)
From the entrance to the village playing field walk along the main road as far as The Marquis of Granby pub. Opposite, on the left of the road, a footpath crosses a brief grass patch, goes over a stile and into a small housing development. In a few paces walk up a tarmac path between houses, and into a field. Walk up the slope alongside a hedge, but when it cuts back to the left continue uphill aiming towards the right-hand end of a tree-and-hedge boundary. A stile is found a few paces from the corner where the footpath winds among trees to reach a narrow road. Bear right for a few paces, then left up a slope among trees to emerge into a steeply sloping meadow. Bear right to a stile in a fence (fine views into the valley) and walk ahead over a hilltop field towards a distant TV transmitter mast.

Pass a little to the right of a bungalow and Lone Barn Farm, and cross a stony drive. Continue in the same direction, go through a gap in the far boundary hedge and over a crossing bridleway. A stile gives access to the next field. Maintain direction (soon gaining a view half-left to Dover Castle seen nearly $4^{1}/_{2}$ miles away) and come onto a narrow lane. Bear slightly right. The lane curves left, slopes downhill, then bends to the right by Fern Cottage. Turn left on a track that leads for about $^{3}/_{4}$ mile to Poulton Farm (Grid ref: 269413) set in a shallow secretive valley.

Enter the farmyard, but just beyond a stone-walled barn on the

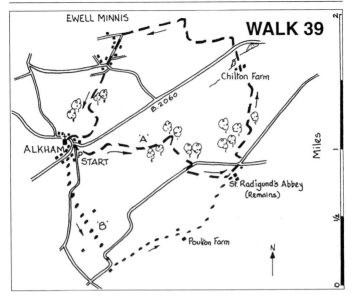

left go through a farm gate (also on the left), bear right and walk along the lower edge of a sloping meadow, gradually rising uphill. Cross a shoulder of hillside into a shallow bowl scooped from the downs, and bear left to its upper edge - which is in the form of a saddle. On the way cross several tracks of a moto-cross circuit. If racing is in progress the continuation of the walk will doubtless be delayed until it is safe to proceed.

Go through a gate and directly ahead across a large hilltop field. The map indicates two paths, but only one was evident during research. If two are found, take the left-hand option leading to a stile in the far boundary. Cross the corner of a second field to a plank footbridge and another stile. Directly ahead is St Radigund's Abbey Farm. Walk ahead and come to a farm drive by a pond (Grid ref: 274419), there to join Route A.

Continued Route: (St Radigund's Abbey - Ewell Minnis - Alkham)
Bear left along the drive to pass the Abbey (1) gatehouse, formerly the church tower, and several other crumbling ruins on the right. At

185

a junction of country roads walk ahead in the direction of River. About 50 yards later turn left on a track which soon becomes a narrow bridleway going into woods. Wander through them for some way, descending after a while, then come out to a cropped downland slope above Chilton Farm. Go down the slope and through the farm, whose drive leads to the B2060.

Cross the road and walk up the bridleway/track opposite. A noticeboard warns that the way passes through army training land. Come to a stony crossing track and bear left, slanting up the hillside. After passing through woods come onto the hilltop crest where the way forks by a cattle grid. Cross a stile next to it and continue ahead parallel with a fence forming the left-hand boundary of the field. On the far side bear left by an oak-crowned tumulus, go through a field gate and walk ahead along a bridleway leading to Ewell Minnis.

At a junction of tracks by a black weatherboarded house (Ewell Cottage) bear left. The track becomes a narrow lane which passes The New Castle Inn. Beyond the pub continue ahead at a lane junction and soon reach a minor crossroads. Take the narrow lane opposite, and in a few paces when it curves to the right cross a stile on the left into a large field. A footpath crosses slightly to the right, and over the brow of hill comes to a stile in the opposite boundary hedge to enter Sladden Wood (2).

Descend through the wood and come out to a coombe of hillside. Wander down, keeping well to the right of a pair of barns, and veer right round the hillside making towards the lower edge of a small woodland. A swing gate leads into the bottom of the woods and a footpath goes alongside a fence. When it forks ignore the left-hand option and continue, now beside a privet hedge. On reaching a very narrow lane bear left for a few paces, then turn right on a continuing footpath sloping down among trees. Veer left alongside gardens and come out on yet another narrow road. Go through a swing gate opposite and over a small meadow to enter Alkham churchyard (3). Leave by the lychgate into the heart of the village.

Items of interest:

1: St Radigund's Abbey. Founded in 1193 by Premonstratensian monks, the Abbey is named after a sixth-century German princess, kidnapped as a child by the King of the Franks, who later forcibly

Oil-seed rape near St Radigund's Abbey swallows all trace of the footpath

married her. In due course she managed to leave him and devoted the rest of her days to the care of "lepers and persons afflicted with the most nauseus distempers". The Abbey stood for three centuries before Henry VIII ordered its demolition in order that the stone could be used to strengthen his defences through the construction of Sandgate Castle near Folkestone. The Elizabethan farmhouse next to the Abbey ruins was built out of the refectory.

2: Sladden Wood. Acquired by the Kent Trust for Nature Conservation in 1991, Sladden Wood Nature Reserve is a grade 1 SSSI. Covering 18 acres of ancient coppiced woodland, among the plants found here are the green hellebore, lady orchid and herb paris.

3: Alkham Church. The thirteenth-century church of St Anthony the Martyr, built by the monks of St Radigund's Abbey, contains the inscribed lid from the coffin of one of the monks. The epitaph is said to be the oldest in any Kent church. It reads: "Here lieth Herbert, offspring of Simon. A man open-hearted, assured by hope of good things, fluent in words of faith." The main feature of the church is its arcaded north chapel.

187

WALK 40: ST MARGARET'S AT CLIFFE - KINGSDOWN - ST MARGARET'S

Distance:	6 miles
Maps:	OS Pathfinder TR 24/34 Dover 1:25,000
	OS Landranger 179 Canterbury & East Kent 1:50,000
Start:	St Margaret's Parish Church (Grid ref: 358447)
Access:	On B2058 about 3 miles north-east of Dover.
Parking:	Public car park immediately south of the church.
Refreshments:	Pubs in St Margaret's at Cliffe and, off route, Kingsdown.

This is a justifiably popular walk along one of the finest stretches of clifftop in Kent. Unlike some coastal paths, this one does not entail a constant helter-skelter course, but offers a gentle, fairly level stroll with views on a clear day to the French coast way across the English Channel. But coastal walking forms only part of the route, for a return is made from Kingsdown on an inland bridleway that in itself has much to commend it.

There are two St Margaret's outside Dover; St Margaret's at Cliffe and St Margaret's Bay. The former has a number of pubs alongside the main street and a splendid Norman church, while St Margaret's Bay is famed as the place from which cross-Channel swimmers traditionally set out for France.

* * *

Walk along the B2058 from St Margaret's at Cliffe (1) heading seaward to St Margaret's Bay (2). After about ³/₄ mile the road makes a sharp right-hand bend with a bungalow on the left (Grid ref: 367445). Immediately before it turn left on a footpath signposted to Kingsdown. The path is dark among trees and follows a high wooden fence. When the fence ends there are one or two access points for the beach, but the footpath continues ahead, still among trees, shrubs and wild clematis, then across the more open National Trust-owned area of The Leas. Much of this clifftop walk is over National Trust land, purchased in 1974 during the Enterprise Neptune campaign, and the path is waymarked for the Saxon Shore Way (3).

Soon pass a tall obelisk (the Dover Patrol Memorial (4)), then a Coastguard Station, beyond which the open clifftop provides marvellous views on a clear day. On coming to wooden bars marking the boundary of the National Trust's Brockhill Farm continue ahead with Walmer and Kingsdown Golf Course seen on the left. Pass a few houses and the Clubhouse, then descend steps to a road near an army rifle range. Walk ahead for about 50 yards, then climb a flight of concrete steps on the left, at the top of which the continuing path is bordered by a wire fence. Still following the fence veer left to pass between the chalets of a holiday camp on one side, and Kingsdown International Scout Campsite on the other.

The footpath emerges to a residential street by the entrance to the Scout Campsite (Grid ref: 376482). Walk directly ahead, and when the street forks take the right branch. At a T junction continue ahead for about 30 yards, then bear left on a bridleway that passes along the end of gardens. When it forks veer left alongside a cypress hedge. Ahead stretch large rolling fields; a big open landscape serenaded by skylarks.

Continue ahead on a clear footpath over the first large field, then alongside a hedge, over a second field and, entering a third, cross to its far left-hand corner to come onto a track. Follow this ahead with East Hill above to the left. It's a peaceful hedge-lined bridleway with fine downland scenery spreading all around, and it leads without com-plication all the

WALK 40

way to the main road by The Red Lion pub in St Margaret's at Cliffe. Turn left and wander alongside the road to the church.

Items of interest:

1: St Margaret's at Cliffe. The church is its noblest building, with one of the largest Norman towers in the county and fine carvings round the west door. It was damaged twice during World War II by enemy shells fired from across the Channel. For 300 years a curfew bell has been rung each night from Michaelmas to Lady Day in response to the plight of a local shepherd who, in 1696, fell over the cliff. A more recent tragedy is recalled in a stained glass window depicting the *Herald of Free Enterprise* which capsized off Zeebrugge in 1988. Three of those who died were crew members from St Margaret's.

2: St Margaret's Bay. Local folklore has it that smugglers adopted the bay for bringing ashore their illicit booty, and it is said that the church tower at St Margaret's at Cliffe was used to store the rope and tackle by which goods were hauled up the cliff-face. During World War II the famous naval guns, nicknamed Winnie and Pooh, were positioned here to fire salvos across the Channel.

3: The Saxon Shore Way. This 140-mile long distance route begins at Gravesend beside the Thames, and finishes at Rye in Sussex, passing along the way numerous fortifications built many centuries ago to defend the county against invading Saxons.

4: The Dover Patrol Memorial. Erected in memory of the men of the Dover Patrol who died in World War I, this tall granite obelisk had its foundation stone laid in 1919 by Prince Arthur of Connaught, and was unveiled two years later by the Prince of Wales. The memorial now also commemorates those who lost their lives defending the Straits of Dover during World War II.

BIBLIOGRAPHY

1: Walking guides:

Kent County Council produces a variety of guides to medium-distance trails, as well as packs of leaflets on country park walks, coastal walks etc. *Kent for Walking* is a booklet which lists scores of walks and associated guides throughout the county. The current edition (£1.50p plus p&p) is available from: Access & Recreation Officer, KCC Planning Department, Springfield, Maidstone ME14 2LX.

The following is a selection of those mentioned above. All are available from the aforementioned KCC address, but check prices first.

Eden Valley Walk by Caroline Wing
Greensand Way in Kent by Bea Cowan
Medway Valley Walk by Kev Reynolds
Stour Valley Walk by G.Allanson, C.Donaldson, R.Lloyd & K.Snelson
Centenary Walks through Kent
Coastal Walks in Kent (White Cliffs)
Coastal Walks in Kent (Wantsum Walks)
Country Park Walks in Kent (Manor Park)
Kent Farm Trails
River Valley Walks in Kent (River Medway)

2: Long distance walks guides:

A number of long-distance trails pass through Kent, most of which are mentioned elsewhere in this book. The following are relevant guidebooks:

London Countryway
A London Countryway by Keith Chesterton (Constable)

North Downs Way
A Guide to the Pilgrims Way and North Downs Way by Christopher John Wright (Constable)
North Downs Way National Trail Guide by Neil Curtis (Aurum Press)
The North Downs Way - A Users Guide by KCC Planning Dept

Saxon Shore Way
The Saxon Shore Way by RA Kent Area
The Saxon Shore Way by Allan Sillitoe and Fay Godwin (Hutchinson)

The Wealdway
The Wealdway and The Vanguard Way by Kev Reynolds (Cicerone Press)
The Wealdway by RA Kent Area

3: General and specific subject guides to Kent:

Libraries and bookshops have a rich collection of books with a Kent background. Walkers wishing to increase their knowledge of the county will find plenty of interest among the following.

Belloc, H.	*The Old Road* (Constable, 1904)
Bignall, A.	*Kent Lore* (Hale, 1983)
	The Kent Village Book (Countryside Books, 1986)

Church, R.	*Kent* (Hale, 1948)
Cobbett, W.	*Rural Rides* (1912 edition)
Davis, P.	*Leisure Guides - Kent* (Hale, 1989)
Glover, J.	*The Place Names of Kent* (Batsford, 1976)
Kaye-Smith, S.	*Weald of Kent and Sussex* (Hale, 1973)
Margary, I.	*Roman Ways in the Weald* (Dent, 1948)
Mason, O.	*South-East England* (Bartholomew, 1979)
Maxwell, D.	*Unknown Kent* (Bodley Head, 1921)
McNay, M.	*Red Guide - Kent* (Waymark Publications/AA, 1989)
Mee, A.	*The King's England - Kent* (Hodder & Stoughton, 1969)
Newman, J.	*North-East and East Kent* - The Buildings of England series, (ed) Pevsner N. (Penguin, 1976)
Reynolds, K.	*The Visitor's Guide to Kent* (Moorland Publishing, 1990)
Spence, K.	*The Companion Guide to Kent and Sussex* (Collins, 1973)
Vigar, J.	*Exploring Kent Churches* (Meresborough, 1985)

Printed by
Carnmor Print & Design, London Road, Preston , UK